Fairy Tale Fun!

Nancy Polette • Illustrations by Paul Dillon

Neal-Schuman Publishers, Inc.

New York   London

Published by Neal-Schuman Publishers, Inc.
100 William St., Suite 2004
New York, NY 10038
http://www.neal-schuman.com

Printed and bound in the United States of America.

The paper used in this publication meets the minimum requirements of American National Standard for Information Sciences—Permanence of Paper for Printed Library Materials, ANSI Z39.48-1992.

Library of Congress Cataloging-in-Publication Data

Polette, Nancy.
  Fairy tale fun! / Nancy Polette ; illustrations by Paul Dillon.
     p. cm.
  Includes bibliographical references and indexes.
  ISBN 978-1-55570-773-6 (alk. paper)
  1. Children's libraries—Activity programs. 2. Storytelling. 3. Tales—Bibliography. 4. Children's films—Catalogs. I. Title.

Z718.3.P65 2012
027.62'51—dc23
                                                                                          2011033984

Table of Contents

Part III: Fairy Tale Bingo

Part IV: Paper Bag Puppet Patterns

Preface

Fairy Tale Fun! will help you introduce children to a world where heroes face witches, trolls and dragons abound, and princesses are imprisoned in towers or sleep for 100 years in magical kingdoms. It's fairy tale fun time with poems, stories, games, treasure hunts, and word searches. Children's librarians, teachers, and anyone doing programming for children in preschool through the elementary grades will find this unique book invaluable.

Why fairy tales, you may ask? This thought-provoking quote from Albert Einstein provides an excellent answer:

> The fairest thing we can experience is the mysterious. It is the fundamental emotion which stands at the cradle of true art and true science. He who knows it not, who can no longer wonder, can no longer feel amazement, is as good as dead, a snuffed-out candle.
>
> —Albert Einstein, *The World as I See It*
> (Citadel Press, 1956, p. 7)

Einstein as a child was an avid reader of fairy tales.

As a Professor of Children's Literature for over forty years and former Director of the Lindenwood University Laboratory School for Gifted Children, I have worked with many very bright children who had little or no knowledge of traditional literature. Children are taught to type before they can read; they visit factories and offices and can use telephones and computers with amazing dexterity. Are we spending as much time emphasizing the quality of the imagination that can grasp the unseen, the intangible? The great Russian writer Kornei Chukovsky gives us food for thought:

> The young child uses fantasy as a means of learning, and adjusts it to reality in the exact amounts his need demands. The present belongs to the cautious, the sober, the routine-prone, but the future belongs to those who do not rein in their imaginations.
>
> —Kornei Chukovsky, *From Two to Five*
> (University of California Press, 1963)

Fairy tales can create a startling new environment for the mind. Once a child has ventured beyond earthly restrictions, he or she can never crawl back into old modes of thought. Fairy tales do relate specifically to contemporary society. Surely Hans Christian Andersen's *The Nightingale* is a powerful comment on what technology could be doing to our values as it outraces conservation of nature.

Fairy Tale Fun contains 38 programs for introducing the world's most-beloved tales. Each program begins with a participation script to be read by the librarian or teacher with the help of the children who have a role to play. Each tale can be read aloud, shared on film, and enhanced with the many follow-up activities provided in this book.

Fairy tales included are from the collections of Charles Perrault, the Grimm Brothers, Joseph Jacobs, Antoine Galland, and Hans Christian Andersen as well as from the pens of Rudyard Kipling and Robert Browning. In Part I, tales from many writers are listed alphabetically. Part II introduces the original tales of Hans Christian Andersen, often called the Father of the Modern Fairy Tale. Very little preparation is required for using the introductory and follow-up activities for each tale.

Whether these tales are enjoyed in the children's room of the public library or in a school setting, the follow-up activities for each tale are designed to extend enjoyment and understanding. The activities for younger children (ages 4–8) include songs and fingerplays. Part IV of the book includes fourteen paper bag puppet patterns that children can use to make puppets for acting out parts of a story that has been shared or in creating their own stories for dramatic play.

Older children (ages 9–12) will enjoy recalling the tale with the "I Have, Who Has" game. These children can also take part in library treasure hunts related to the tales, which will help children to use skills in locating materials and to become acquainted with library resources. Take-home word searches based on the tales can be enjoyed by parents and children alike. *Fairy Tale Fun!* also includes as Part III a Fairy Tale Bingo game that utilizes clues from many different tales.

Various editions of the tales are readily available. The bibliography for each tale includes print and film versions as well as a listing of free YouTube videos. Brief information about each film is given, including title, running time, producer, and distributor.

Memorized facts are often obsolete by the time children leave school. Imaginative literature, however, can lead children to creative, imaginative thought, which may prove to be all of the education that is lasting. Nothing can replace that spaciousness of vision, that feeling of oneness with mankind, of the universality of life's joys and woes that can come from the pages of inspired writers. The ultimate goal of *Fairy Tale Fun!* is to help librarians, teachers, parents, and caregivers to bring together the minds, spirits, and hearts of children with traditional tales to stimulate the imagination and foster a lifelong love affair with reading and literature.

PART I

TALES FROM MANY LANDS

Aesop's Fables

The Grasshopper and the Ants
The Lion and the Mouse
The Town Mouse and the Country Mouse
The Hare and the Tortoise

(The following can also be done orally, with the children raising their hands to respond.)

Find Someone Who!

Discover what your group has in common with the characters and places in *Aesop's Fables*. Find a different name in the class or group for each item. The winner is the first to complete all eight items. The winner will then read each item and the person whose name is on each line will stand to verify that he or she can actually qualify for the item.

Find someone who . . .

1. Has shared his or her lunch with another person. _____

2. Has seen a squirrel bury food for winter. _____

3. Can name a story where a small character helps a large character. _____

4. Has seen a real lion. _____

5. Can name three dangers found in a city. _____

6. Can name three dangers found in the country. _____

7. Has won a race. _____

8. Can tell what a FABLE is. _____

Storyteller's Introduction to *Aesop's Fables*

Read these rhymes before showing the film or reading the fables.

The Grasshopper and the Ants
In summertime busy ants
Stored winter food away,
But grasshopper did not store
Instead he chose to play.
When winter came
He asked the ants
To give him food and drink.
Do you believe the ants should share?
Tell us what you think.

(Encourage children's responses.)

The Lion and the Mouse
A mighty lion
Was most upset.
Hunters had caught him
In a net.
A mouse scurried by
Quick as a wink.
Will mouse help lion?
What do you think?

(Encourage children's responses.)

The Town Mouse and the Country Mouse
A mouse from town was offered
A feast of cheese and bread,
But he refused to eat it
Preferred town food instead.
Took his cousin to the city,
And as they feasted there
A huge black cat attacked them
And gave them quite a scare.

*(Encourage children's responses. Would you
rather eat a meal with the town mouse or the
country mouse?)*

The Hare and the Tortoise
One day a hare was telling
How fast that he could go
And made fun of the tortoise
Whose pace was very slow.
The tortoise asked the hare
To take part in a race.
Hare laughed at poor old tortoise,
Told him "You will take last place."
The race began and speedy hare
Took off quick as a wink.
Now who will win the race?
Tell us what you think.

(Encourage children's responses.)

Aesop's Fables: The Films

Alpha Home Entertainment, prod. 2009. *Aesop's Fables.* Black-and-white film. 90 minutes. Ages 4–8. Contains several fables. Available from Amazon.com.

Golden Books Publishers, prod. 1989. *The Hare and the Tortoise/The Vain Crow.* Full-color animated film. 30 minutes. Ages 4–6. Faithful retelling of the fables. Available from Amazon.com.

Golden Books Publishers, prod. 1991. *Aesop's Fables: The Ant and the Grasshopper/Wind and the Sun.* Full-color animated film. 30 minutes. Ages 4–6. Faithful retelling of the fables. Available from Amazon.com.

Imada, Chiaki, prod. 1997. *Aesop's Fables.* Full-color animated film. 1 hour. Ages 4–8. Introduces several fables. Available from Amazon.com.

Questar, prod. 2008. *The Country Mouse and the City Mouse.* Full-color animated film. 120 minutes. Ages 5–10. Extended retelling of the fable. Available from Amazon.com.

Free online video of *The Lion and the Mouse* available here: http://www.youtube.com/watch?v=SXYW0blGk4w, running time 5:05.

Aesop's Fables: The Books

Ash, Russell, and Bernard Higton, comps. 1990. *Aesop's Fables.* San Francisco: Chronicle Books.

Brett, Jan. 1994. *Town Mouse and the Country Mouse.* New York: Putnam.

Cech, John. 2009. *Aesop's Fables.* Illustrated by Martin Jarrie. New York: Sterling.

Herman, Gail. 2010. *The Lion and the Mouse.* Illustrated by Lisa McCue. New York: Random House.

Lynch, Tom, illus. 2000. *Aesop's Fables.* New York: Viking.

McClintock, Barbara. 1991. *Animal Fables from Aesop.* Boston: Godine.

Morpurgo, Michael. 2005. *The McElderry Book of Aesop's Fables.* Illustrated by Emma Chichester Clark. New York: McElderry Books.

Orgel, Doris. 2000. *The Lion and the Mouse: And Other Aesop's Fables.* Illustrated by Bert Kitchen. New York: Dorling Kindersley.

Pinkney, Jerry, illus. 2000. *Aesop's Fables.* New York: SeaStar Books.

Pinkney, Jerry, illus. 2009. *The Lion and the Mouse.* New York: Little, Brown and Company.

Shirley, Alice. 2009. *Aesop's Fables.* London: Pavilion Children's Books.

Sneed, Brad. 2003. *Aesop's Fables.* New York: Dial Books for Young Readers.

Wallner, John. 1987. *City Mouse and Country Mouse and Two More Mouse Tales from Aesop.* New York: Scholastic.

Winter, Milo, illus. 1994. *Aesop for Children.* New York: Scholastic.

Zwerber, Lisbeth, illus. 2006. *Aesop's Fables.* New York: North-South.

Aesop's Fables: Songs for Younger Children

The Lion and the Mouse / The Town Mouse and the Country Mouse
(Tune: "Have You Ever Seen a Lassie?")

If I could be a lion,
A lion, a lion,
If I could be a lion,
I'd sound just like this!
(Children roar.)

If I could be a little mouse,
A little mouse, a little mouse,
If I could be a little mouse,
I'd sound just like this!
(Children squeak.)

Grasshopper and the Ants
(Tune: "The Muffin Man")

Yes, I am the grasshopper,
The grasshopper, the grasshopper.
Yes, I am the grasshopper.
I like to dance and play.

Yes, we are the busy ants,
The busy ants, the busy ants.
Yes, we are the busy ants.
We store our food away.

The Tortoise and the Hare
(Tune: "Are You Sleeping")

Slowpoke tortoise, slowpoke tortoise
Plods along, plods along.
Silly hare is sleeping.
Tortoise keeps on walking.
Who will win? Sing this song.

Aesop's Fables: I HAVE, WHO HAS Game

Directions: Cut all the cards apart. Each player gets one card. Begin with the question preceded by an asterisk (*). The student with the answer card responds.

I HAVE: Country Mouse saw a big cat so she ran back home to the country where she was safe. *WHO HAS: What did the worker ants and grasshopper do in the summer?	I HAVE: Tortoise challenged hare to a race. WHO HAS: How did tortoise win the race?
I HAVE: In the summer the worker ants gathered food for the winter while grasshopper played. WHO HAS: What penalty did grasshopper pay for playing all summer?	I HAVE: Hare played and napped while tortoise took one step after another, never stopping. WHO HAS: When town mouse visited country mouse what foods was she offered?
I HAVE: Grasshopper had no food when winter came. WHO HAS: What did mouse promise lion if the lion did not eat him?	I HAVE: Country mouse offered town mouse nuts and grains. WHO HAS: How did town mouse feel about this simple fare?
I HAVE: Mouse promised lion to help him one day. WHO HAS: How did mouse keep his promise?	I HAVE: Town mouse declared that the town food was much better and invited country mouse for a visit. WHO HAS: What did country mouse find in town?
I HAVE: Mouse chewed a hole in the net to let lion escape. WHO HAS: When hare bragged about how fast he could run, what did tortoise do?	I HAVE: Country mouse found a grand feast with jellies and cakes. WHO HAS: What else did country mouse find?

Aesop's Fables: Library Treasure Hunt

Go to the children's nonfiction shelves. Look for each number on the spine of the books. What is each book about? That is the missing word. Write it on the line after the number. The player who finds all of the missing words first is the winner.

1. Grasshopper liked to play and 792.8. _____	2. The ants spent the summer storing their 613.2. _____
3. The lion was helped by a 599.35. _____	4. The 599.75 is King of the Jungle. _____
5. Hare is another name for 599.3. _____	6. Country mouse was frightened by a 636.8. _____

Key: 1. dance; 2. food; 3. mouse; 4. lion; 5. rabbit; 6. cat

Aesop's Fables: Word Search

N	G	S	R	R	O	E	H	A	R	E
N	T	E	U	N	E	A	L	H	S	N
R	T	C	I	O	N	E	E	I	P	O
P	L	Y	R	T	N	U	O	C	S	A
O	O	T	S	A	N	T	S	O	Y	A
S	O	T	P	T	R	T	E	N	L	E
R	E	P	P	O	H	S	S	A	R	G
N	T	S	T	L	U	L	H	A	M	R
H	E	O	Y	O	T	I	E	R	O	T
O	P	T	M	N	W	O	O	A	O	S
A	S	S	O	E	T	N	U	T	H	S

Words to find:

tortoise	grasshopper	hare
ants	town	country
mouse	lion	net

Aladdin and the Wonderful Lamp

(The following can also be done orally, with the children raising their hands to respond.)

Find Someone Who!

Discover what your group has in common with the characters and places in *Aladdin and the Wonderful Lamp*. Find a different name in the class or group for each item. The winner is the first to complete all eight items. The winner will then read each item and the person whose name is on each line will stand to verify that he or she can actually qualify for the item.

Find someone who . . .

1. Can name a Middle Eastern country. _____

2. Has seen a magic show. _____

3. Has explored a cave. _____

4. Knows what a genie is. _____

5. Has lost something valuable. _____

6. Has a first or last name that begins with the letter A. _____

7. Can name another story with a happy ending. _____

8. Can name another story with a magic object. _____

Storyteller's Introduction to *Aladdin and the Wonderful Lamp*

Cut apart the cards on the next page. Assign one card to each of three groups. Groups practice saying their card. When the storyteller holds the card up, each group responds in turn.

Storyteller:
Aladdin, Aladdin,
Poor young scamp.
Magician asks,
"Retrieve my lamp."
Foolish boy,
Feeling brave,
Climbs into
A deep dark cave.
Trapped inside,
Ill at ease,
Finds the lamp.
Magician flees.

Group (1):
Aladdin, Aladdin,
Lucky scamp,
Now he owns
The magic lamp.

Storyteller:
Genie appears,
Sets him free,
Every wish
Will guarantee.
Wife trades lamp
One fateful hour,
Knowing nothing
Of its power.
Wishes made
Come true no more.
Once again
Aladdin's poor.

Group (2):
Aladdin, Aladdin,
Unlucky scamp,
Now he's lost
The magic lamp.

Storyteller:
WAIT!
Aladdin has
A magic ring.
Wishing will
A genie bring.
Powers less
Than magic lamp,
Still the genie
Helps the scamp.
Boy gives up
His selfish ways.
Now he will
See better days.
Genie hears
The boy's petition,
Uses powers,
Defeats magician.

Group (3):
Aladdin, Aladdin,
Lucky scamp,
Owns again
The magic lamp.

All (1)

Aladdin, Aladdin,

Lucky scamp,

Now he owns

The magic lamp.

All (2)

Aladdin, Aladdin,

Unlucky scamp,

Now he's lost

The magic lamp.

All (3)

Aladdin, Aladdin,

Lucky scamp,

Owns again

The magic lamp.

Aladdin and the Wonderful Lamp: The Films

Clements, Ron, and John Musker, prods. 1992. *Aladdin.* Directed by Ron Clements and John Musker. Voices of Scott Weinger, Robin Williams, Linda Larkin, Jonathan Freeman, Frank Welker, Gilbert Gottfried, Douglas Seale. Animated color film. 90 minutes. Ages 7–12. Follows the story line with addition of musical numbers. Updated for DVD release 2004. Distributed by Walt Disney Studios Home Entertainment.

Eskinazi, Diane, and Golden Films, prods. 1992. *Aladdin.* Directed by Masakazu Higuchi and Chinami Namba. Puppet-animated color film. 49 minutes. Ages 7–12. Follows the basic story line. Released on DVD 2002. Distributed by Good Times Home Entertainment.

Greatest Tales, prod. 1977. *Aladdin and His Wonderful Lamp.* Animated color film. 9 minutes. Ages 4–8. A highly condensed version of the tale, appropriate for younger children. Distributed by Phoenix/BFA Films and Video.

Lion's Gate Films, prod. 1985. *Aladdin and His Wonderful Lamp.* Starring Valerie Bertinelli, Robert Carradine, James Earl Jones, Leonard Nemoy. Live action color film. 60 minutes. Ages 7–12. Distributed by Fox Video.

Free viewing on the Internet via MSN video: *Aladdin and His Wonderful Lamp*, http://www.bing.com/videos/watch/video/aladdin-and-his-wonderful-lamp/17we9sk6l, running time 48:04, ages 5–8.

Aladdin and the Wonderful Lamp: The Books

Carrick, Carol. 1989. *Aladdin and the Wonderful Lamp.* Illustrated by Donald Carrick. New York: Scholastic.

Cloke, Rene. 1984. *Aladdin and His Wonderful Lamp.* N.p.: Exeter Books.

Eastman, Kevin. 1996. *Aladdin and the Wonderful Lamp.* Mahwah, NJ: Troll.

Kimmel, Eric A. 1992. *The Tale of Aladdin and the Wonderful Lamp: A Story from the Arabian Nights.* Illustrated by Ju-Hong Chen. New York: Holiday House.

Lang, Andrew, ed. 1969. *The Arabian Nights Entertainment*, 295–315. Mineola, NY: Dover.

Lang, Andrew. 2008. *Stories from 1001 Arabian Nights.* St. Petersburg, FL: Red and Black Publishers.

Lang, Andrew, and Errol Le Cain. 1983. *Aladdin and the Wonderful Lamp.* New York: Puffin.

Philip, Neil. 1994. *The Arabian Nights.* London: Orchard Books.

Pullman, Philip. 2005. *Aladdin and the Enchanted Lamp.* Illustrated by Sophy Williams. New York: Arthur A. Levine Books.

Ransome, Arthur, and T. Blakeley Mackenzie. 2010. *Aladdin and His Wonderful Lamp in Rhyme.* Charleston, SC: Nabu Press.

Ray, Jane, illus. 2000. "Aladdin and the Enchanted Lamp," in *Fairy Tales Told by Berlie Doherty.* Somerville, MA: Candlewick Press.

Robinson, W. Heath, illus. 1993. *Aladdin and Other Tales from the Arabian Nights.* New York: Knopf.

Tarnowska, Wafa'. 2010. *The Arabian Nights.* Illustrated by Carole Hénaff. Cambridge, MA: Barefoot Books.

White, Ann Terry. 1953. *Aladdin and the Wonderful Lamp.* New York: Random House.

Aladdin and the Wonderful Lamp: I HAVE, WHO HAS Game

Directions: Cut all the cards apart. Each player gets one card. Begin with the question preceded by an asterisk (*). The student with the answer card responds.

I HAVE: Aladdin lost his castle and all his riches. *WHO HAS: Where did Aladdin live?	I HAVE: He was trapped in the cave. WHO HAS: How did Aladdin escape from the cave?
I HAVE: Aladdin lived in China. WHO HAS: Who pretended to be Aladdin's uncle?	I HAVE: Aladdin escaped with the help of the genie of the ring. WHO HAS: What did the lamp give Aladdin and his mother?
I HAVE: The magician pretended to be Aladdin's uncle. WHO HAS: Where did the magician ask Aladdin to go?	I HAVE: The lamp gave them riches. WHO HAS: Whom did Aladdin marry?
I HAVE: The magician asked Aladdin to go into an underground cave. WHO HAS: What did the magician give Aladdin?	I HAVE: Aladdin married the Sultan's daughter. WHO HAS: What did the Sultan's daughter do with the lamp?
I HAVE: The magician gave Aladdin a magic ring. WHO HAS: What happened to Aladdin in the cave?	I HAVE: The Sultan's daughter gave the magician the old lamp for a new lamp. WHO HAS: What happened when the lamp was lost?

Aladdin and the Wonderful Lamp: Library Treasure Hunt

Go to the children's nonfiction shelves. Look for each number on the spine of the books. What is each book about? That is the missing word. Write it on the line after the number. The player who finds all of the missing words first is the winner.

1. The country where Aladdin lived is 951.05. _____	2. Aladdin found the lamp in a 551.4. _____
3. The magic fruit was made of 745.58. _____	4. Aladdin asked the genie to build a 728.8. _____
5. A magician makes 793.8. _____	6. Some magicians have a talking 636.6. _____

───────────────────

Key: 1. China; 2. cave; 3. jewels; 4. castle; 5. magic; 6. parrot

Aladdin and the Wonderful Lamp: Word Search

I	F	C	D	A	I	T	M
A	A	R	P	G	A	E	G
H	L	M	U	G	F	C	N
N	A	I	C	I	G	A	M
L	D	N	W	N	T	V	U
A	D	P	I	L	A	E	I
L	I	R	U	H	W	A	L
I	N	S	G	I	C	F	D

Words to find:

Aladdin	magician	China
cave	lamp	fruit
sultan	wife	ring

Beauty and the Beast

(The following can also be done orally, with the children raising their hands to respond.)

Find Someone Who!

Discover what your group has in common with the characters and places in *Beauty and the Beast*. Find a different name in the class or group for each item. The winner is the first to complete all eight items. The winner will then read each item and the person whose name is on each line will stand to verify that he or she can actually qualify for the item. Items can be presented orally with children raising their hands to respond.

Find someone who . . .

1. Has a rose bush growing at home.   _____

2. Has traveled more than 5 miles from
   home.   _____

3. Has been homesick.   _____

4. Has two sisters.   _____

5. Can name another tale with a palace.   _____

6. Can name two words that rhyme with
   BEAST.   _____

7. Can name another tale with an enchanted
   prince.   _____

8. Can name a synonym for BEAUTY.   _____

Storyteller's Introduction to *Beauty and the Beast*

When the storyteller raises his or her right hand, the audience responds, "How nice!" When the storyteller raises his or her left hand, the audience responds, "Oh, dear!"

At the end of the story the storyteller says "Hip! Hip!" and the audience responds with "Hooray! Hooray! Hooray!"

Storyteller:
A father asked his daughters what gifts he might bring them when he returned from a journey. The oldest girls asked for jewels. The youngest daughter asked for a rose.

Group:
How nice!

Storyteller:
On his way home, the man saw a hedge of roses and picked just one when a terrible voice said, "Who told you that you might gather my roses? Nothing now will save you from the death you deserve!"

Group:
Oh, dear!

Storyteller:
The father explained that the rose was for Beauty, his youngest daughter, and that he meant no harm.

"You shall live," the Beast said, "If Beauty will come to my palace and live with me willingly."

Group:
Oh, dear!

Storyteller:
The father returned home and told Beauty what had happened. Since it was her request for the rose that had put her father's life in danger, she agreed to go willingly to the castle of the Beast.

Group:
How nice!

Storyteller:
At first she was frightened, but the Beast treated her kindly. After several months, Beauty asked to be allowed to visit her family and promised to return after two months. But, she broke her promise!

Group:
Oh, dear!

Storyteller:
When she finally returned, she found the Beast near death. Realizing that she loved him, she promised to marry him if he recovered. Lo and behold, no sooner had she made the promise than a spell was broken and the Beast became a handsome prince. Beauty and the Beast lived happily ever after.

Storyteller:
Hip! Hip!

Group:
Hooray! Hooray! Hooray!

Beauty and the Beast: The Films

Alexovich, David, prod. 1990. *Beauty and the Beast.* Animated color film. 12 minutes. Ages 4–8. Condensed rapid-action film. Distributed by Britannica.

Bosustow Entertainment, prod. 1981. *Beauty and the Beast.* Voices of Michael York, Claire Bloom, and James Earl Jones. Animated color film. 12 minutes. Ages 4–8. Distributed by Churchill Media.

Duvall, Shelley, prod. 1983. *Beauty and the Beast.* Faerie Tale Theatre. Starring Klaus Kinski and Susan Sarandon. Live action color film. 50 minutes. Ages 6–10. Distributed by Fox Video.

Greatest Tales, prod. 1980. *Beauty and the Beast.* Animated color film. 11 minutes. Ages 6–10. Follows the basic story outline. Distributed by Phoenix/BFA Films and Video.

Greene, Joshua M., prod. 1988. *Beauty and the Beast.* Narrated by Mia Farrow. Animated color film. 27 minutes. Ages 4–8. This film has won many awards. Distributed by Lightyear Entertainment.

Hahn, Don, and Walt Disney Studios, prods. 1991. *Beauty and the Beast.* Voices of Robby Benson, Jerry Orbach, Angela Lansbury, David Ogden Stiers. Animated color film. 84 minutes. Ages 8–adult. With the addition of musical numbers, it tells the story from the viewpoint of the Beast. Distributed by Walt Disney Pictures. Available on DVD from Amazon.com and Barnes&Noble.com.

Free full-length viewing from Veoh.com: *Beauty and the Beast*, Golden Films, http://www.veoh.com/watch/v15846438PYE6aJ9t, running time 50:00.

Beauty and the Beast: The Books

Beaumont, Jeanne-Marie. 2010. *Beauty and the Beast.* Illustrated by Walter Crane. Seattle, WA: CreateSpace.

Brett, Jan. 1989. *Beauty and the Beast.* New York: Clarion Books.

Eilenberg, Max. 2006. *Beauty and the Beast.* Illustrated by Angela Barrett. Somerville, MA: Candlewick Press.

Gerstein, Mordicai. 1989. *Beauty and the Beast.* New York: Dutton.

Jones, Christianne C. 2005. *Beauty and the Beast.* Illustrated by Amy Bailey Muehlenhardt. Mankato, MN: Picture Window Books.

Mayer, Mariana. 1978. *Beauty and the Beast.* New York: Four Winds Press.

Mills, J. Elizabeth. 2003. *Beauty and the Beast.* Illustrated by Barbara Lanza. New York: Scholastic.

Sabuda, Robert. 2010. *Beauty and the Beast: A Pop-Up Book of the Classic Fairy Tale.* New York: Little Simon.

Titlebaum, Ellen. 2002. *Disney's Beauty and the Beast: A Read-Aloud Storybook.* New York: Random House.

Yep, Laurence. 1997. *Dragon Prince: A Chinese Beauty and the Beast Tale.* Illustrated by Kam Mak. New York: HarperCollins.

Beauty and the Beast: A Song for Younger Children

A Flower Song
(Tune: "The More We Get Together")

Beauty got a flower,
A flower, a flower.
Beauty got a flower.
What kind would it be?
A rose or a tulip, a pansy or lilac?
Beauty got a flower.
What kind would it be?
Beauty got a box of fruit,
A box of fruit, a box of fruit.
Beauty got a box of fruit.
What kind would it be?
Bananas or apples, oranges or peaches?
Beauty got a box of fruit.
What kind would it be?

(Substitute other things Beauty might have received.)
Beauty got some clothing . . .
Beauty got some games to play . . .

Beauty got (a/some) _____, _____, _____.

Beauty got (a/some) _____.
What kind would (it/they) be?
_____ or _____, _____ or _____.
Beauty got (a/some) _____.
What kind would (it/they) be?

Beauty and the Beast: I HAVE, WHO HAS Game

Directions: Cut all the cards apart. Each player gets one card. Begin with the question preceded by an asterisk (*). The student with the answer card responds.

I HAVE: The spell was broken and the Beast became a handsome prince. *WHO HAS: What did Beauty's sisters ask their father to bring them?	I HAVE: Beauty agreed to go to the Beast's castle. WHO HAS: How was Beauty treated at the Beast's castle?
I HAVE: The sisters asked for precious jewels. WHO HAS: What did Beauty ask for?	I HAVE: Beauty was treated kindly at the castle. WHO HAS: What favor did Beauty ask of the Beast?
I HAVE: Beauty asked for a rose. WHO HAS: What happened when the father picked a rose from a garden?	I HAVE: Beauty asked the Beast to let her visit her family for two months. WHO HAS: What happened when Beauty stayed with her family longer than two months?
I HAVE: The Beast who owned the garden threatened the father with death. WHO HAS: To avoid death, what was the father asked to do?	I HAVE: The Beast became so ill he was near death. WHO HAS: What did Beauty do when she returned and found the Beast near death?
I HAVE: The Beast asked the father for one of his daughters, who must come willingly. WHO HAS: Which daughter agreed to go to the castle of the Beast?	I HAVE: She told the Beast she loved him. WHO HAS: What happened when Beauty agreed to marry the Beast?

Beauty and the Beast: Library Treasure Hunt

Go to the children's nonfiction shelves. Look for each number on the spine of the books. What is each book about? That is the missing word. Write it on the line after the number. The player who finds all of the missing words first is the winner.

1. Beauty's sisters asked their father to bring them 745.58. _____	2. Beauty asked her father to bring her a 582.13. _____
3. The Beast lived in a 728.8. _____	4. Beauty's father traveled on a 636.1. _____
5. Beauty wanted to visit her 306.8. _____	6. 793.8 turned the prince into a beast. _____

Key: 1. jewels; 2. flower; 3. castle; 4. horse; 5. family; 6. Magic

Beauty and the Beast: Word Search

P	A	R	H	T	R	I	T
E	A	F	S	U	N	G	E
I	C	A	A	I	A	A	G
B	E	A	U	T	Y	R	C
B	S	S	L	E	H	D	H
F	P	S	O	A	T	E	A
E	C	N	I	R	P	N	R
R	R	F	S	K	E	R	M

Words to find:

beauty	rose	father
beast	palace	prince
charm	kiss	garden

The Boy Who Cried Wolf

(The following can also be done orally, with the children raising their hands to respond.)

Find Someone Who!

Discover what your group has in common with the characters and places in *The Boy Who Cried Wolf.* Find a different name from the class or group for each item. The winner is the first to complete all eight items. The winner will then read each item and the person whose name is on each line will stand to verify that he or she can actually qualify for the item.

Find someone who . . .

1. Has seen a real sheep. _____

2. Has seen a real wolf. _____

3. Has walked in a meadow. _____

4. Has one brother. _____

5. Has lost something valuable. _____

6. Has a first or last name that begins with the letter A. _____

7. Can name another story with a happy ending. _____

8. Can name another story with a magic object. _____

Storyteller's Introduction to *The Boy Who Cried Wolf*

Storyteller:
Boys and girls, when I raise my hand I want you to shout "WOLF!" three times. Ready? Then we will begin.

There was once a young boy named Tom who was very lazy. His job each day when the sun came up was to take the sheep to the meadow to eat the thick, green grass.

"Stay awake," his parents told him. "Watch out for the hungry wolves who can make a tasty meal out of a sheep."

One afternoon, with nothing to do, Tom thought of a fun game. He would see what would happen when he called, *(Storyteller raises hand.)*

Children:
WOLF! WOLF! WOLF!

Storyteller:
The villagers came running and found Tom laughing and the sheep quite safe.

"Do not do that again," they warned. But sure enough, Tom thought it was such a fun game that the next day he shouted, *(Storyteller raises hand.)*

Children:
WOLF! WOLF! WOLF!

Storyteller:
The villagers came running and found Tom laughing and the sheep quite safe.

"Enough is enough," they told the boy. "We will not come running again!"

A few days later, the clouds cast a shadow, the wild birds gave a warning, and hungry wolves came creeping from the trees, their eyes on the fat sheep.

The frightened boy shouted as loudly as he could, *(Storyteller raises hand.)*

Children:
WOLF! WOLF! WOLF!

Storyteller:
But the villagers ignored his cries. Some ate their supper, others did their chores. No one came to help, and many many sheep were killed by the wolves. And, dear children, what do you suppose happened to Tom?

Let's watch the film *(or read the story)* and see.

The Boy Who Cried Wolf: The Films

Buchbinder, Paul, prod. 1983. *The Boy Who Cried Wolf.* Animated color film. 17 minutes. Ages 6–10. No narration. Distributed by Britannica.

Diamond Entertainment, prod. 1991. *The Boy Who Cried Wolf and Other Fabulous Fables.* Animated color film. 33 minutes. Ages 5–8. Available on VHS only from Amazon.com and Barnes&Noble.com.

Greatest Tales, prod. 1981. *The Boy Who Cried Wolf.* Animated color film. 11 minutes. Ages 6–10. A good adaptation of the story. Distributed by Phoenix/BFA Films and Video.

Phoenix Learning Group, prod. 2008. *The Boy Who Cried Wolf.* Animated color film. 11 minutes. Ages 4–8. Available on DVD from Amazon.com and Barnes&Noble .com.

Free viewing on the Internet via YouTube: *Boy Who Cried Wolf,* http://www.youtube .com/watch?v=heasnJY8HMM, running time 4:03.

The Boy Who Cried Wolf: The Books

Alley, Zoë B. 2008. *There's a Wolf at the Door.* Illustrated by R.W. Alley. New York: Roaring Brook Press.

Berendes, Mary. 2010. *The Boy Who Cried Wolf.* Illustrated by Nancy Harrison. North Mankato, MN: Child's World.

Blair, Eric. 2004. *The Boy Who Cried Wolf.* Illustrated by Dianne Silverman. Mankato, MN: Picture Window Books.

The Boy Who Cried Wolf: Student Reader. 1998. New York: Rigby.

Hartman, Bob. 2002. *The Wolf Who Cried Boy.* Illustrated by Tim Raglin. New York: Putnam's Sons.

Hennessy, Barbara. 2006. *The Boy Who Cried Wolf.* Illustrated by Boris Kulikov. New York: Simon and Schuster.

Littledale, Freya. 1987. *The Boy Who Cried Wolf.* New York: Scholastic.

Mackinnon, Mairi, Mike Gordon, and Carl Gordon. 2008. *The Boy Who Cried Wolf.* London: Usborne.

Rocco, John. 2007. *Wolf! Wolf!* New York: Hyperion Books for Children.

Ross, Tony. 1992. *The Boy Who Cried Wolf.* New York: Puffin Books.

Schecter, Ellen. 1994. *The Boy Who Cried Wolf.* Stamford, CT: Weekly Reader.

Wildish, Lee. 2008. *The Boy Who Cried Wolf.* I'm Going to Read Series. New York: Sterling.

Worley, Rob M. 2010. *The Boy Who Cried Wolf.* Illustrated by Will Meugniot. Edina, MN: Magic Wagon.

The Boy Who Cried Wolf: Activities for Younger Children

Ask:

What does a real wolf look like?

How big is a wolf?

Where does it live?

Show picture books about real wolves.

Play HELP ME!

———————————————

HELP ME!

Directions: Read the poem aloud. When you come to a rhyming word, say, "Help Me!" and allow the children to add the missing word.

Lazy Tom went to the meadow

To care for all the sheep.

Lazy Tom gave a yawn,

Laid down and went to "HELP ME!" _____. (*sleep*)

Wolves came by and saw the sheep

And thought that they would steal

Two or three and take them home

To have them for their "HELP ME!" _____. (*meal*)

The boy woke up and saw the wolves,

Let out a mighty cry,

But no one came to help him.

Now don't you wonder "HELP ME!" _____? (*why*)

The Boy Who Cried Wolf: I HAVE, WHO HAS Game

Directions: Cut all the cards apart. Each player gets one card. Begin with the question preceded by an asterisk (*). The student with the answer card responds.

I HAVE: Tom shouted for help but no one came. *WHO HAS: What one word best describes Tom?	I HAVE: Tom shouted "Wolf! Wolf! Wolf!" WHO HAS: What did the villagers find when they came to help Tom?
I HAVE: The word that describes Tom is lazy. WHO HAS: What was Tom's job.	I HAVE: The villagers found there was no wolf. WHO HAS: How did the villagers feel about the trick Tom played on them?
I HAVE: Tom was to look after the sheep. WHO HAS: Where did Tom take the sheep?	I HAVE: The villagers were angry. WHO HAS: What happened when Tom shouted "Wolf! Wolf! Wolf!" a second time?
I HAVE: Tom took the sheep to the meadow. WHO HAS: What two things did Tom's parents tell him to do?	I HAVE: The villagers came running and found there was no wolf. WHO HAS: What did the villagers tell Tom.
I HAVE: Tom's parents told him to stay awake and watch out for wolves. WHO HAS: What did Tom shout?	I HAVE: The villagers told Tom they would not come a third time. WHO HAS: What happened when the wolves really did attack the sheep?

The Boy Who Cried Wolf: Library Treasure Hunt

Go to the children's nonfiction shelves. Look for each number on the spine of the books. What is each book about? That is the missing word. Write it on the line after the number. The player who finds all of the missing words first is the winner.

1. Tom went to the meadow when the 525 came up. _____	2. Tom's job was to watch the 636.3. _____
3. The 551.57 cast a shadow on the meadow. _____	4. The hungry 599.77 wanted to eat the sheep. _____
5. The 598 gave a warning. _____	6. The wolves came creeping out of the 582.16. _____

_____

Key: 1. sun; 2. sheep; 3. clouds; 4. wolves; 5. birds; 6. trees

The Boy Who Cried Wolf: Word Search

T	F	O	O	L	O	M	Y
W	O	L	F	D	E	O	A
O	S	W	N	A	B	K	T
D	C	H	N	N	E	C	P
A	P	E	E	G	R	I	W
E	L	P	O	E	P	R	I
M	T	L	O	R	P	T	O
E	E	P	A	M	G	A	O

Words to find:

boy   sheep   meadow

trick   wolf   town

people   danger   fool

The Bremen Town Musicians

(The following can also be done orally, with the children raising their hands to respond.)

Find Someone Who!

Discover what your group has in common with the characters and places in *The Bremen Town Musicians*. Find a different name from the class or group for each item. The winner is the first to complete all eight items. The winner will then read each item and the person whose name is on each line will stand to verify that he or she can actually qualify for the item.

Find someone who . . .

1. Can name a popular tune.   _____

2. Can play a musical instrument.   _____

3. Has visited an empty house.   _____

4. Has taken a walk in the woods.   _____

5. Has sung before a group.   _____

6. Has a dog or cat for a pet.   _____

7. Has seen a rooster on a farm.   _____

8. Can name another word for ROBBER.   _____

Storyteller's Introduction to *The Bremen Town Musicians*

Before presenting the story, assign animal sounds to the audience: Donkey, Hee-Haw; Cat, Meow; Dog, Ruff Ruff; Rooster, Cock-a-Doodle Do. At a signal from the storyteller, the audience members make the appropriate sounds.

Storyteller: Walking along the road to Bremen Town were four animals who were so old that their owners found they were no longer useful.

The cat (**Audience:** MEOW) could no longer catch mice.

The dog (**Audience:** RUFF RUFF) did no good in the hunt.

The donkey (Audience: HEE-HAW) could not carry heavy loads.

The rooster's *owner* planned to cook him in a stew (**Audience:** COCK-A-DOODLE-DO).

So they decided to travel together to Bremen Town and earn their living by becoming musicians.

When night came, they spied a small cottage in the woods with a light in the window. They peeked in to see four robbers eating a fine meal.

The donkey (**Audience:** HEE-HAW) placed his forefeet on the window sill.

The dog (**Audience:** RUFF RUFF) climbed on the donkey's back.

The cat (**Audience:** MEOW) climbed on top of the dog.

The rooster (**Audience:** COCK-A-DOODLE-DO) perched on the cat's head.

Then they all performed their music at the same time. (**Audience, loudly:** HEE-HAW, RUFF RUFF, MEOW, COCK-A-DOODLE-DO). The robbers, thinking it was a goblin, fled into the woods.

Later that night, one robber returned to see if the cottage was empty. As soon as he entered the dark room, the cat (**Audience:** MEOW) flew into his face spitting and scratching. The dog (**Audience:** RUFF RUFF) bit his leg, the donkey (**Audience:** HEE-HAW) kicked him, and the rooster crowed (**Audience:** COCK-A-DOODLE-DO).

The robber fled in terror to tell his companions about the terrible witch who had attacked him. The robber never again went near the cottage, and the animals never made it to Bremen, for they found the cottage in the woods an excellent place to live out their days.

Audience: MEOW, HEE-HAW, RUFF RUFF, COCK-A-DOODLE-DO.

The Bremen Town Musicians: The Films

East West Entertainment, prod. 1959. *The Bremen Town Musicians.* Animated color film. 77 minutes. Ages 6–10. Faithful to the original tale with two bonus features. Available from Amazon.com.

Good Times Video, prod. 2006. *The Bremen Town Musicians.* Animated color film. 50 minutes. Ages 6–10. Follows the story line with some added features. Available on DVD from Amazon.com.

Greatest Tales, prod. 1981. *The Bremen Town Musicians.* Animated color film. 16 minutes. Ages 5–8. Characters and background are Asian. Distributed by Phoenix/BFA Films and Video.

Institut für Film und Bild, prod. 1972. *The Bremen Town Musicians.* Animated color film. 16 minutes. Ages 5–10. Uses puppet animation. Distributed by Films, Inc.

Rabbit Ears Productions, prod. 1994. *The Bremen Town Musicians.* Animated color film. 30 minutes. Ages 6–10. Faithful retelling of the Grimm tale. Available from Amazon.com.

Free viewing on the Internet via YouTube: *The Bremen Town Musicians*, http://www.youtube .com/watch?v=v1q4MGCX_ms, running time 8:27.

The Bremen Town Musicians: The Books

Blair, Eric. 2010. *Bremen Town Musicians.* Illustrated by Bill Dickson. Mankato, MN: Picture Window Books.

Brothers Grimm. 2007. *The Bremen Town Musicians.* Illustrated by Lisbeth Zwerger. New York: Miniedition.

Diamond, Donna. 1981. *Bremen Town Musicians.* New York: Delacorte.

Grimm, Gebrüder. 1993. *Town Musicians of Bremen: A Grimm's Fairy Tale.* Edinburgh, UK: Floris.

Hillert, Margaret. 2007. *Four Good Friends.* Illustrated by Krystyna Stasiak. Chicago: Norwood House Press.

Johnson, David. 2005. *Bremen Town Musicians.* New York: Spotlight.

Kruss, Kestutis Kasparavicius. 1988. *The Bremen Town-Musicians.* Esslingen, DU: Esslinger.

Lai, Hsin-Shih. 2007. *The Bremen Town Musicians.* Illustrated by Howard Kirk Besserman. Great Barrington, MA: Bell Pond Books.

Orgel, Doris. 2004. *The Bremen Town Musicians.* Illustrated by Bert Kitchen. New York: Roaring Brook.

Plume, Ilse. 1980. *The Bremen Town Musicians.* New York: Doubleday.

Price, Kathy. 2002. *The Bourbon Street Musicians.* Illustrated by Andrew Glass. New York: Clarion Books.

Puttapipat, Niroot. 2005. *The Musicians of Bremen.* Somerville, MA: Candlewick Press.

Shub, Elizabeth. 1980. *The Bremen Town Musicians.* New York: Morrow

Stevens, Janet, illus. 1992. *The Bremen Town Musicians.* New York: Holiday House.

Watts, Bernadette. 1992. *The Bremen Town Musicians.* New York: North-South Books.

Zens, Patricia Martin, and Charles Mikolaycak. 1964. *The Bremen-Town Musicians.* New York: Merrigold Press.

The Bremen Town Musicians: A Song for Younger Children

Sing Like the Bremen Town Musicians!

(Tune: "You Are My Sunshine")

I have a donkey.
He's my pet donkey.
He is my best friend
Both night and day.
I have a donkey.
He's my pet donkey.
Please don't take my donkey away.

I have a rooster.
He's my pet rooster.
He is my best friend
Both night and day.
I have a rooster.
He's my pet rooster.
Please don't take my rooster away.

I have a frisky dog.
He's my pet frisky dog.
He is my best friend
Both night and day.
I have a frisky dog.
He's my pet frisky dog.
Please don't take my frisky dog away.

I have a fat cat.
She's my pet fat cat.
She is my best friend
Both night and day.
I have a fat cat.
She's my pet fat cat.
Please don't take my fat cat away.

The Bremen Town Musicians: I HAVE, WHO HAS Game

Directions: Cut all the cards apart. Each player gets one card. Begin with the question preceded by an asterisk (*). The student with the answer card responds.

I HAVE: The animals made the cottage in the woods their home. *WHO HAS: Why did the donkey's master want to get rid of him?	I HAVE: The animals decided to travel to Bremen Town and become musicians. WHO HAS: What did the animals find in the forest?
I HAVE: The donkey was too old to carry heavy loads. WHO HAS: Why did the dog's master want to get rid of him?	I HAVE: They found a cottage with robbers inside. WHO HAS: How did the animals frighten the robbers away?
I HAVE: The dog was too old to keep up with the hunt. WHO HAS: Why did the cat's master want to get rid of him?	I HAVE: They stood on top of each other and made a terrible noise. WHO HAS: What happened when a robber went back to the dark cottage?
I HAVE: The cat was too old to catch mice. WHO HAS: What did the rooster's master plan to do with him?	I HAVE: The robber was attacked by the animals. WHO HAS: What did the robber say had attacked him?
I HAVE: The rooster's master planned to cook him in a stew. WHO HAS: What did the animals decide to do?	I HAVE: The robber said an awful witch had attacked him. WHO HAS: What did the animals do?

The Bremen Town Musicians: Library Treasure Hunt

Go to the children's nonfiction shelves. Look for each number on the spine of the books. What is each book about? That is the missing word. Write it on the line after the number. The player who finds all of the missing words first is the winner.

1. An old donkey who was running away met a 636.7 on the road. _____	2. A dog and a donkey met a 636.8 on the road. _____
3. The cat was so old she could no longer catch 599.35. _____	4. The noisiest of the animals was the 636.5. _____
5. The animals found a 690 in the woods. _____	6. The animals decided to live together in the 577.3. _____

Key: 1. dog; 2. cat; 3. mice; 4. rooster; 5. house; 6. forest

The Bremen Town Musicians: Word Search

S	N	E	M	E	R	B
H	R	O	G	R	E	S
C	I	E	W	M	T	O
T	A	R	B	G	S	D
I	H	T	T	B	O	B
W	Y	E	K	N	O	D
G	I	A	N	T	R	R

Words to find:

donkey	dog	cat
rooster	Bremen	robbers
witch	ogre	giant

Cinderella

(The following can also be done orally, with the children raising their hands to respond.)

Find Someone Who!

Discover what your group has in common with the characters and places in *Cinderella*. Find a different name from the class or group for each item. The winner is the first to complete all eight items. The winner will then read each item and the person whose name is on each line will stand to verify that he or she can actually qualify for the item.

Find someone who . . .

1. Has two sisters. _____

2. Has a fireplace at home. _____

3. Has dressed up for a party. _____

4. Can name a fairy tale with a prince. _____

5. Likes pumpkin pie. _____

6. Can name a Mother Goose rhyme with mice. _____

7. Has a first or last name that begins with the letter C. _____

8. Has lost a shoe. _____

Storyteller's Introduction to *Cinderella*

At a signal from the storyteller, the children repeat the phrase "They worked Cinderella from morning till night."

Storyteller:
Three sisters lived
in a house in the city.
Two were ugly,
Cinderella was pretty.
The sisters were jealous,
And so out of spite . . .

Children:
They worked Cinderella
From morning till night.

Storyteller:
When last days of summer
Turned into fall,
The king of the land
Was giving a ball.
Their gowns must be lovely,
Their gowns must be right, so . . .

Children:
They worked Cinderella
From morning till night.

Storyteller:
She stitched and she stitched,
The gowns to enhance.
Then off went the sisters
To the palace to dance,
Left a mess to be cleaned up
And things to put right, so . . .

Children:
They worked Cinderella
From morning till night

Storyteller:
She pulled out her hankie
To catch a big tear,
When to her surprise
What should appear,

But a vision so strange
That her eyes opened wide,
For there was her godmother
Right by her side.
She told the poor girl that
It just isn't right that . . .

Children:
They worked Cinderella
From morning till night.

Storyteller:
"You are pretty," she said,
And dainty and small,
So here is a gown,
You will go to the ball.
At the risk of seeming
A bit impolite,
You must hurry away
At the stroke of midnight.
So she danced with the prince
In her ball gown so new,
But in leaving at midnight
The girl lost her shoe.
She went straight to the cottage
And back to her plight where . . .

Children:
They worked Cinderella
From morning till night.

Storyteller:
Will the prince find his partner,
His true love so sweet,
As he tries the glass slipper
On hundreds of feet?
To find out the answer,
To be in the know,
Come now take my hand,
To the movies we'll go.

Cinderella: The Films

Alexovich, David, prod. 1990. *Cinderella*. Color animated film. 12 minutes. Ages 4–8. Follows the story line with humor added. Distributed by Britannica.

Dubin, Charles S., prod. 1964. *Rodgers and Hammerstein's Cinderella*. Starring Lesley Ann Warren and Ginger Rogers. Live action color film. 84 minutes. Ages 6–10. Released on DVD 2003. Distributed by Fox Video. Available on DVD from Amazon.com and Barnes&Noble.com.

Duvall, Shelley, prod. 1984. *Cinderella*. Faerie Tale Theatre. Starring Jennifer Beals, Matthew Broderick, Jean Stapleton. Live action color film. 60 minutes. Ages 6–adult. Excellent production, faithful to the original tale. Distributed by Fox Video.

Jackson, Brian, prod. 1987. *Cinderella*. Color animated film. 17 minutes. Ages 5–10. Animated drawings faithfully re-create the tale. Distributed by Barr Films.

New York State Theatre Institute, prod. 1998. *A Tale of Cinderella*. Starring Christianne Tisdale, Joel Aroeste, Sean Sullivan, Lorraine Serabian. Live action color film. 129 minutes. Ages 6–adult. An excellent production. Released on DVD 2004. Distributed by Warner Home Video.

Walt Disney, prod. 1950. *Cinderella*. Narrated by Betty Lou Gerson. Voiced by Ilene Woods, Verna Felton, James MacDonald, Don Barclay. Color animated film. 75 minutes. Ages 4–12. Animal characters and musical numbers added to the basic story. Distributed by Buena Vista Home Video. Available on DVD from Amazon.com and Barnes&Noble.com.

Free viewing on the Internet via YouTube: *Fairy Tales—Cinderella*, http://www.youtube.com/watch?v=hebtX_RMdFw, running time 4:35.

Cinderella: The Books

Bell, Anthea, trans. 1999. *Cinderella*. Illustrated by Loek Ko. New York: North-South Books.

Brown, Marcia. 1954. *Cinderella or the Little Glass Slipper*. New York: Scribners.

Climo, Shirley. 1992. *The Egyptian Cinderella*. Illustrated by Ruth Heller. New York: HarperCollins.

Climo, Shirley. 1999. *The Persian Cinderella*. Illustrated by Robert Florczak. New York: HarperCollins.

Climo, Shirley. 2006. *The Korean Cinderella*. Illustrated by Ruth Heller. New York: HarperCollins.

dePaola, Tomie. 2002. *Adelita: A Mexican Cinderella Story*. New York: G.P. Putnam's Sons.

Eilenberg, Max. 2008. *Cinderella*. Illustrated by N. Sharkey. Somerville, MA: Candlewick Press.

Grimes, Nikki. 2002. *Walt Disney's Cinderella*. Illustrated by Don Williams and Jim Story. New York: Random House.

Hillert, Margaret. 1970. *Cinderella at the Ball*. Illustrated by Janet LaSalle. Cleveland, OH: Modern Curriculum Press.

Knight, Hilary. 2001. *Hilary Knight's Cinderella*. New York: Random House.

Kraft, K. Y., illus. 2000. *Cinderella*. New York: SeaStar Books.

Kurtz, John. 2005. *Cinderella*. New York: Jump at the Sun.

McClintock, Barbara. 2005. *Cinderella*. New York: Scholastic.

Rylant, Cynthia. 2007. *Walt Disney's Cinderella*. Illustrated by Mary Blair. White Plains, NY: Disney Press.

Sanderson, Ruth. 2008. *Cinderella*. New York: Little, Brown and Company.

Cinderella: A Song for Younger Children

This Is the Way . . . Just Like Cinderella

(Tune: "Here We Go 'Round the Mulberry Bush")
(Children make the motions as they sing the song.)

This is the way we iron the clothes,
Iron the clothes, iron the clothes.
This is the way we iron the clothes,
Just like Cinderella.

This is the way we scrub the floor,
Scrub the floor, scrub the floor.
This is the way we scrub the floor,
Just like Cinderella.

This is the way we wash the windows,
Wash the windows, wash the windows.
This is the way we wash the windows,
Just like Cinderella.

This is the way we dust and sweep,
Dust and sweep, dust and sweep.
This is the way we dust and sweep,
Just like Cinderella.

This is the way we dance away,
Dance away, dance away.
This is the way we dance away,
Just like Cinderella.

Cinderella: I HAVE, WHO HAS Game

Directions: Cut all the cards apart. Each player gets one card. Begin with the question preceded by an asterisk (*). The student with the answer card responds.

I HAVE: Cinderella was the owner of the slipper. *WHO HAS: How did Cinderella's stepsisters treat her?	I HAVE: A fairy godmother appeared to Cinderella. WHO HAS: How did the fairy godmother help Cinderella?
I HAVE: Her stepsisters treated her like a servant. WHO HAS: How was Cinderella clothed and fed?	I HAVE: She gave her a ball gown and sent her to the ball in a coach. WHO HAS: What warning did the godmother give Cinderella?
I HAVE: Cinderella wore rags and was not given enough to eat. WHO HAS: What message did the king's messengers bring?	I HAVE: The godmother told Cinderella she must be home by midnight. WHO HAS: What did Cinderella lose when she left the ball?
I HAVE: The messengers brought news of a ball to be held on the Twelfth Night. WHO HAS: How did the stepsisters prepare for the ball?	I HAVE: Cinderella lost her glass slipper. WHO HAS: Who found the slipper and what did he do?
I HAVE: They tried on many gowns and kept Cinderella up all night sewing. WHO HAS: What happened to Cinderella when the stepsisters went to the ball?	I HAVE: The prince found the slipper and set out to find the owner. WHO HAS: Who did the prince find was the owner of the slipper?

Cinderella: Library Treasure Hunt

Go to the children's nonfiction shelves. Look for each number on the spine of the books. What is each book about? That is the missing word. Write it on the line after the number. The player who finds all of the missing words first is the winner.

1. Cinderella lived in the kitchen with rats and 599.35. —————————————	2. The stepsisters tried on many gowns and 745.58. —————————————
3. The ball was to be held at the king's 728.8. —————————————	4. The godmother used 793.8 to create Cinderella's ball gown. —————————————
5. The godmother turned the mice into 636.1. —————————————	6. Cinderella was the 523.8 of the ball. —————————————

—————————————————————

Key: 1. mice; 2. jewels; 3. castle; 4. magic; 5. horses; 6. star

Cinderella: Word Search

I	M	T	H	G	H	S	L	T	L
E	I	E	G	O	G	N	H	E	W
E	G	S	E	D	H	C	M	T	P
R	R	S	P	M	A	S	D	H	I
E	E	R	G	O	W	N	O	G	P
A	P	G	C	T	G	T	H	I	R
R	P	I	M	H	I	N	T	N	I
S	I	S	T	E	R	S	E	D	N
A	L	L	E	R	E	D	N	I	C
E	S	L	L	A	B	O	G	M	E

Words to find:

Cinderella	godmother	gown
ball	prince	slipper
coach	midnight	sisters

The Elephant's Child

(By Rudyard Kipling)

(The following can also be done orally, with the children raising their hands to respond.)

Find Someone Who!

Discover what your group has in common with the characters and places in *The Elephant's Child*. Find a different name from the class or group for each item. The winner is the first to complete all eight items. The winner will then read each item and the person whose name is on each line will stand to verify that he or she can actually qualify for the item.

Find someone who . . .

1. Can find Africa on a map. _____

2. Who has an aunt and an uncle. _____

3. Can name a river. _____

4. Can name two kinds of melons. _____

5. Has seen a real crocodile. _____

6. Has seen a python at the zoo. _____

7. Can name two uses for an elephant's trunk. _____

8. Can name another of the *Just So Stories* by Rudyard Kipling. _____

Storyteller's introduction to *The Elephant's Child*

When the storyteller says, "For he was full of . . ." the audience will respond with the words "SATIABLE CURIOSITY."

Storyteller:
One morning the elephant's child,
Who was difficult to ignore,
Asked his aunts and uncles
A question never asked before:
He asked:
"'Scuse me! What does the crocodile have
    for dinner?"
For he was full of . . .

Audience:
"SATIABLE CURIOSITY"

Storyteller:
He asked his mother and his father
And his uncle and his aunt,
Who refused to give an answer
Perhaps because they can't,
But he kept on with his question,
Never taking time for thanking
Those relatives he bothered.
Instead he got a spanking
For he was full of . . .

Audience:
"SATIABLE CURIOSITY"

Storyteller:
The next morning it was chilly,
Enough to make him shiver,
So he started on a journey
To the green Limpopo River.
A huge bicolored snake
Called "Hello there" as he passed.
He stopped and looked it in the eye.
This question he then asked:
"'Scuse me! What does the crocodile have
    for dinner?"
For he was full of . . .

Audience:
"SATIABLE CURIOSITY"

Storyteller:
The slimey snake uncoiled
And stretched from scale to scale.
He raised up from his rock and
Spanked the elephant with his tail.
Poor elephant!
No one would answer his question,
Even when he said please,
So the elephant walked beside the river,
Lined with fever trees,
Till he met another creature,
A creature with a smile.
The elephant's child did not know
This was the crocodile.
He asked:
"'Scuse me! What does the crocodile have
    for dinner?"
For he was full of . . .

Audience:
"SATIABLE CURIOSITY"

Storyteller:
The crocodile gave a wink,
And from the river he rose,
Opened wide his musky mouth
And grabbed the elephant's nose.
The rock snake grabbed the elephant
The crocodile wanted for dinner.
He pulled in the other direction
But no one was the winner.
Now the elephant has a very long nose
That's not about to shrink.
Should he have been so curious?
Tell us what you think.

The Elephant's Child: The Films

Coronet, prod. 1984. *Elephant's Child.* Animated color film. 12 minutes. Ages 4–8. Faithful to the original tale. Distributed by Coronet/MTI Film and Video.

LCA, prod. 1970. *How the Elephant Got Its Trunk.* Animated color film. 7 minutes. Ages 4–8. Faithful to the original tale. Distributed by Coronet/MTI Film and Video.

Rabbit Ears Productions, prod. 1986. *The Elephant's Child.* Narrated by Jack Nicholson. Iconographic, full-color film showing pages from the book illustrated by Tim Raglin and published in 1985 by Knopf. 30 minutes. Ages 4–8. Distributed by Random House Home Video.

Two free online animated shorts available on YouTube: http://www.youtube.com/watch?v=E0rTWq4qT74, running time 4:25, and http://www.youtube.com/watch?v=6smTRZRanpk, running time 10:28.

The Elephant's Child: The Books

Corr, Christopher, illus. 2004. *A Collection of Rudyard Kipling's Just So Stories.* Somerville, MA: Candlewick.

Kipling, Rudyard. 1996. *The Elephant's Child.* Illustrated by Lorinda Bryan Cauley. New York: Harcourt.

Kipling, Rudyard. 1996. *Just So Stories.* Illustrated by Barry Moser. New York: Morrow.

Kipling, Rudyard. 2001. *Just So Stories.* N.p.: Dover.

Kipling, Rudyard. 2006. *The Elephant's Child.* Illustrated by Jan Mogensen. Northampton, MA: Crocodile Books.

Kipling, Rudyard. 2009. *Just So Stories.* Edison, NJ: Chartwell Books.

Lewis, Lisa. 2009. *Just So Stories: For Little Children.* New York: Oxford University Press.

Lisle, Janet Taylor. 2002. *Just So Stories.* New York: Simon and Schuster.

Rowe, John A., illus. 1995. *The Elephant's Child.* New York: North-South Books.

Stroud, Jonathan. 2008. *Just So Stories.* New York: Penguin.

The Elephant's Child: An Activity for Younger Children

Walking in the Jungle

Gather picture books about each of these animals: elephant, hippopotamus, giraffe, ostrich, python, baboon, crocodile. Be sure there is a picture of the animal on the cover.

Hold up a book about elephants.

Ask the children:

"Walking in the jungle, what do I see?"

The children respond:

"I see an ELEPHANT looking at me."

Hold up a book about a hippopotamus.

Ask the children:

"Walking in the jungle, what do I see?"

The children respond:

"I see a hippopotamus looking at me."

Hold up a book about a giraffe.

Ask the children:

"Walking in the jungle, what do I see?"

The children respond:

"I see a giraffe looking at me."

Follow the pattern for other animals in the story: ostrich, python, baboon, crocodile.

The Elephant's Child: I HAVE, WHO HAS Game

Directions: Cut all the cards apart. Each player gets one card. Begin with the question preceded by an asterisk (*). The student with the answer card responds.

I HAVE: He found many new uses for it. *WHO HAS: Where did the elephant's child live?	I HAVE: The crocodile grabbed the elephant child's nose to pull him into the water. WHO HAS: What did the crocodile plan to do with the elephant's child?
I HAVE: The elephant's child lived in Africa. WHO HAS: Why was he spanked by his aunts and uncles?	I HAVE: The crocodile planned to have the elephant's child for dinner. WHO HAS: Who rescued the elephant's child?
I HAVE: He asked too many questions. WHO HAS: What question did he ask that he had never asked before?	I HAVE: The rock snake rescued the elephant's child. WHO HAS: How did the elephant's child get a long nose?
I HAVE: He asked, "What does the crocodile have for dinner?" WHO HAS: Why did he not know the crocodile when he met one?	I HAVE: When the snake and crocodile pulled in different directions, the nose got longer and longer. WHO HAS: How long did the elephant's child wait for his nose to shrink?
I HAVE: The elephant's child had never seen a crocodile. WHO HAS: How did the crocodile answer the elephant child's question?	I HAVE: He waited three days, but the nose did not shrink. WHO HAS: Why was the elephant's child not unhappy about his new nose?

The Elephant's Child: Library Treasure Hunt

Go to the children's nonfiction shelves. Look for each number on the spine of the books. What is each book about? That is the missing word. Write it on the line after the number. The player who finds all of the missing words first is the winner.

1. The elephant's child lived in 960. _____	2. The Kolokolo 598 told him to go to the river banks. _____
3. The elephant's child walked beside the Limpopo 577.6. _____	4. He met a large green 597.96. _____
5. The river was all set about with fever 582.16. _____	6. He did not know what a 597.98 looked like. _____

Key: 1. Africa; 2. bird; 3. River; 4. snake; 5. trees; 6. crocodile

The Elephant's Child: Word Search

B	L	O	B	A	B	O	O	N
E	I	R	I	A	R	E	S	H
L	I	R	H	I	C	H	T	O
E	L	I	D	O	C	O	R	C
P	H	E	F	F	A	R	I	G
H	D	I	S	S	A	E	C	B
A	C	I	P	O	T	R	H	E
N	B	I	E	P	N	C	N	P
T	R	U	N	K	O	P	N	O

Words to find:

elephant	trunk	nose
ostrich	giraffe	hippo
baboon	bird	crocodile

The Elves and the Shoemaker

(The following can also be done orally, with the children raising their hands to respond.)

Find Someone Who!

Discover what your group has in common with the characters and places in *The Elves and the Shoemaker*. Find a different name from the class or group for each item. The winner is the first to complete all eight items. The winner will then read each item and the person whose name is on each line will stand to verify that he or she can actually qualify for the item.

Find someone who . . .

1. Can find Germany on a map. _____

2. Has left work to be finished later. _____

3. Has written a thank-you letter. _____

4. Has made a wish on a star. _____

5. Has paid more for an item than it was worth. _____

6. Has kept a secret. _____

7. Has kept a promise. _____

8. Has done a good deed for another person. _____

Storyteller's Introduction to *The Elves and the Shoemaker*

Children join in on this repeating phrase: "Hammer, hammer, stitch and sew, tap, tap, tap."

Storyteller: One night a poor shoemaker cut out the last leather he had to make one pair of shoes. He would finish the shoes in the morning.

But late that night, who should appear but two tiny elves, and guess what they did!

Children:
Hammer, hammer, stitch and sew, tap, tap, tap.
Hammer, hammer, stitch and sew, tap, tap, tap.

Storyteller: That's right. The elves hammered and sewed and made a beautiful pair of shoes. Then they scampered off into the night.

Imagine the shoemaker's surprise the next morning to find the new shoes ready for a customer. In fact, the customer paid enough for the shoes that the shoemaker was able buy leather for two pairs of shoes, which he cut out that night before he went to bed. Guess what happened! Two tiny elves appeared and . . .

Children:
Hammer, hammer, stitch and sew, tap, tap, tap.
Hammer, hammer, stitch and sew, tap, tap, tap.

Storyteller: Night after night, whatever was laid out in the evening was finished by morning. One night the shoemaker and his wife watched to see who had brought them such good fortune, and sure enough they saw the little elves and heard . . .

Children:
Hammer, hammer, stitch and sew, tap, tap, tap.
Hammer, hammer, stitch and sew, tap, tap, tap.

Storyteller: "Look," said the wife. "They have no clothes." That night the wife sewed two little suits and left them out for the elves, who were so delighted that they . . .

What do you suppose they did? Let's watch the film *(or listen to the story)* to find out.

The Elves and the Shoemaker: The Films

Coronet, prod. 1962. *The Shoemaker and the Elves*. Animated film with puppets. 13 minutes. Ages 4–10. A faithful adaptation. Distributed by Coronet/MTI Film and Video.

Hanna-Barbera and Hallmark, prods. 1990. *The Elves and the Shoemaker*. Introduced by Olivia Newton-John. Animated color film. 30 minutes. Ages 4–8. Some material added to the original tale. Distributed by Hanna-Barbera Home Video.

Institut für Film und Bild, prod. 1971. *The Shoemaker and the Elves*. Animated film with puppets. 15 minutes. Ages 4–10. A faithful adaptation. Distributed by Films, Inc.

Turner Home Entertainment, prod. 1997. *Timeless Tales: Elves and Shoemaker*. Animated color film. 30 minutes. Ages 4–8. Available on VHS from Amazon.com and Barnes&Noble.com.

Free viewing on the internet via YouTube: *Fairy Tales—The Shoe Maker and the Elves*, http://www.youtube.com/watch?v=4T5j61Ii4dM, running time 3:50, and http://www.youtube.com/watch?v=cTPIPeCBzeY, running time 9:27.

The Elves and the Shoemaker: The Books

Arengo, Sue, and Adam Stower. 2001. *The Shoemaker and the Elves*. New York: Oxford University Press.

Bailey, J. 1989. *The Elves and the Shoemaker*. New York: Steck Vaughn.

Cech, John. 2007. *The Elves and the Shoemaker*. Illustrated by Kirill Chelushkin. New York: Sterling.

Crook, Marie, and Jacqui Campbell. 2000. *The Elves and the Shoemaker*. New York: Penguin.

Galdone, Paul. 1984. *The Elves and the Shoemaker*. New York: Clarion Books.

Golden Books. 1983. *The Elves and the Shoemaker*. Racine, WI: Western Publishing.

LaMarche, Jim. 2007. *The Elves and the Shoemaker*. San Francisco: Chronicle Books.

Littledale, Freya, and Brinton Turkle. 1992. *The Elves and the Shoemaker*. New York: Scholastic.

Page, Nick, and Claire Page. 2009. *The Elves and the Shoemaker*. Illustrated by Sara Baker. Berkhamsted, UK: Make Believe Ideas.

Rowland, Jada. 1989. *The Elves and the Shoemaker*. Chicago, IL: Contemporary Books.

Southgate, Vera. 2006. *The Elves and the Shoemaker*. London: Ladybird Books.

Stein, Meg. 2001. *The Elves and the Shoemaker*. Marlborough, MA: Sundance Publications.

Thibault, Dominque, illus. 2001. *The Elves and the Shoemaker: A Fairy Tale by the Brothers Grimm*. Little Pebbles Book Series. New York: Abbeville Kids.

The Elves and the Shoemaker: A Song for Younger Children

This Is What a _____ Does
(Tune: "The Muffin Man")

(Gather books about workers and community helpers.
Hold the books up one at a time.)

This is what a <u>shoemaker</u> does,
A <u>shoemaker</u> does,
A <u>shoemaker</u> does.
This is what a <u>shoemaker</u> does.
A <u>shoemaker</u> makes our shoes.

This is what a <u>baker</u> does,
A <u>baker</u> does,
A <u>baker</u> does.
This is what a <u>baker</u> does.
A <u>baker</u> bakes our bread.

This is what a <u>carpenter</u> does,
A <u>carpenter</u> does,
A <u>carpenter</u> does.
This is what a <u>carpenter</u> does.
A <u>carpenter</u> builds our house.

This is what a <u>doctor</u> does,
A <u>doctor</u> does,
A <u>doctor</u> does.
This is what a <u>doctor</u> does.
A <u>doctor</u> makes us well.

The Elves and the Shoemaker: I HAVE, WHO HAS Game

Directions: Cut all the cards apart. Each player gets one card. Begin with the question preceded by an asterisk (*). The student with the answer card responds.

I HAVE: The elves put the suits on and danced out the door. *WHO HAS: In what country did the shoemaker and his wife live?	I HAVE: The customer paid twice what he usually would have paid. WHO HAS: What did the shoemaker do with the money?
I HAVE: The shoemaker and his wife lived in Germany. WHO HAS: How do we know the shoemaker was poor?	I HAVE: He bought enough leather to make two pairs of shoes. WHO HAS: What did the elves do?
I HAVE: The shoemaker and his wife went to bed hungry. WHO HAS: Why could the shoemaker not make and sell many shoes?	I HAVE: The elves came every night to finish the shoes. WHO HAS: What did the curious shoemaker and his wife do?
I HAVE: The shoemaker had only enough leather to make one pair of shoes. WHO HAS: What happened when he left his work to be finished in the morning?	I HAVE: The shoemaker and his wife watched one night to see the elves working on the shoes. WHO HAS: What did the shoemaker and his wife do to show their thanks?
I HAVE: Two elves came at night and finished the shoes. WHO HAS: What did the customer do to show how pleased he was with the shoes?	I HAVE: They made the elves new suits. WHO HAS: What did the elves do when they found the new suits?

The Elves and the Shoemaker: Library Treasure Hunt

Go to the children's nonfiction shelves. Look for each number on the spine of the books. What is each book about? That is the missing word. Write it on the line after the number. The player who finds all of the missing words first is the winner.

1. The shoemaker lived in the country of 943. _____	2. The shoes were made out of 675. _____
3. The elves began their work when the 523.8 came out. _____	4. Elves are 793.8 people. _____
5. The shoemaker's wife made 391 for the elves. _____	6. The elves were so happy they did a 792.8. _____

—————————————————

Key: 1. Germany; 2. leather; 3. stars; 4. magic; 5. clothes; 6. dance

The Elves and the Shoemaker: Word Search

L	R	E	E	T	E	A	S	S
A	R	E	L	C	M	A	H	R
A	H	E	M	V	L	O	T	O
R	E	K	A	M	E	O	H	S
A	I	R	S	S	A	S	R	S
E	R	A	A	P	T	H	E	I
T	O	H	H	A	H	M	A	C
E	O	D	O	C	E	E	D	S
M	C	C	H	R	R	A	R	A

Words to find:

leather	shoes	scissors
elves	shoemaker	hammer
coats	caps	

The Fisherman and His Wife

(The following can also be done orally, with the children raising their hands to respond.)

Find Someone Who!

Discover what your group has in common with the characters and places in *The Fisherman and His Wife*. Find a different name from the class or group for each item. The winner is the first to complete all eight items. The winner will then read each item and the person whose name is on each line will stand to verify that he or she can actually qualify for the item.

Find someone who . . .

1. Has caught a fish.   _____

2. Has seen a real ocean.   _____

3. Likes to eat carrots.   _____

4. Can name two other garden vegetables.   _____

5. Knows what a flounder is.   _____

6. Can name another tale with a selfish person. _____

7. Has been caught outside in a storm.   _____

8. Has made a wish that did not come true.   _____

Storyteller's Introduction to *The Fisherman and His Wife*

Cut apart the cards on the next page. The children take the part of the wife and respond when a card is held up.

Storyteller: A fisherman and his wife live in a snug little hut by the sea. The fisherman spends his days catching fish and his wife tends her garden of cabbages and carrots. Imagine the fisherman's surprise one day when he catches a magic flounder! This magic flounder could talk and promised to grant the fisherman a wish if he would let the fish go. The fisherman asked his wife what they should wish for.

Wife: Go and tell the fish a large cottage is my wish.

Storyteller: That is just what the fisherman did and the wish was granted. He thought it was a very fine cottage indeed. But the wife was not happy.

Wife: Go and tell the fish a castle is my wish.

Storyteller: That is just what the fisherman did and the wish was granted. He thought it was a very fine castle indeed. But the wife was not happy.

Wife: Go and tell the fish to be queen is my wish.

Storyteller: She also wished that her husband should become an emperor. But the magic fish did not grant the wish. In fact, the fish created a great storm and took away all the wishes it had granted. What do you suppose the wife will do now? Let's watch the film *(or listen to the story)*.

Go and tell the fish
a large cottage is my wish.

Go and tell the fish
a castle is my wish.

Go and tell the fish
to be queen is my wish.

The Fisherman and His Wife: The Films

Bosustow Productions, prod. 1977. *The Fisherman and His Wife.* Animated color film. 10 minutes. Ages 4–8. Faithful to the original tale. Distributed by Churchill Media.

Rabbit Ears Productions, prod. 1994. *The Fisherman and His Wife.* Voices of Jodie Foster, Meryl Streep, Dennis Hopper. Animated color film. 30 minutes. Ages 6–10. Faithful to the original tale. Distributed by Sony Pictures. Available from Amazon .com and Barnes&Noble.com.

Time Life, prod. 2000. *The Fisherman and His Wife.* Animated color film. Ages 4–8. This version will appeal to Hispanic children. Available from Amazon.com and Barnes&Noble.com.

Weston Woods, prod. 1970. *The Fisherman and His Wife.* Partially animated color film. 20 minutes. Ages 4–8. Features only the voice of the storyteller. Faithful to the original tale. Distributed by Weston Woods.

Free viewing on the internet via YouTube: *Grim Tales—The Fisherman and His Wife,* http://www.youtube.com/watch?v=boRowDEAJ7Y, running time 10:59. Free viewing of Bosustow production via YouTube: http://www.youtube.com/watch?v= 5SOqJgbo1nc, running time 10:28.

The Fisherman and His Wife: The Books

Arengo, Sue. 2001. *The Fisherman and His Wife.* Illustrated by Annabelle Hartman. New York: Oxford UP.

Blair, Eric. 2004. *The Fisherman and His Wife: A Retelling of the Grimms' Fairy Tale.* Illustrated by Todd Ouren. Mankato, MN: Coughlan.

Chardiet, Bernice. 1993. *The Magic Fish.* Rap Tales. Illustrated by Sam Viviano. New York: Scholastic.

Demi, illus. 1995. *The Magic Gold Fish: A Russian Folktale.* New York: Henry Holt.

Gagliardi, Maria Francesca. 1969. *The Magic Fish.* London: MacDonald.

Isadora, Rachel. 2008. *The Fisherman and His Wife.* New York: Putnam's Sons.

Littledale, Freya. 1992. *The Magic Fish.* New York: Scholastic.

Luzzati, Emanuele. 1972. *Punch and the Magic Fish: A Grimm Brothers' Tale.* New York: Random House.

Metaxas, Eric, and Diana Bryan. 2005. *The Fisherman and His Wife.* Madison, NC: Spotlight Books.

Stewig, John Warren. 1988. *The Fisherman and His Wife.* Illustrated by Margot Tomes. New York: Holiday House.

Wells, Rosemary. 1998. *The Fisherman and His Wife.* Illustrated by Eleanor Hubbard. New York: Dial Books for Young Readers.

The Fisherman and His Wife: A Song for Younger Children

The Poor Man Had a Greedy Wife
(Tune: "Mary Had a Little Lamb")

(1)

The poor man had a greedy wife,
A greedy wife, a greedy wife,
The poor man had a greedy wife.
She asked for a new _____.
(rhymes with mouse)

(2)

The poor man had a greedy wife,
A greedy wife, a greedy wife.
The poor man had a greedy wife.
She asked for a new _____.
(rhymes with hassle)

(3)

The poor man had a greedy wife,
A greedy wife, a greedy wife.
The poor man had a greedy wife.
She asked to become _____.
(rhymes with seen)

Encourage children to think of more things the greedy wife would ask for:

She asked for a <u>new hat</u>.
She asked for a <u>new car</u>.
She asked for a <u>diamond necklace</u>.

The Fisherman and His Wife: I HAVE, WHO HAS Game

Directions: Cut all the cards apart. Each player gets one card. Begin with the question preceded by an asterisk (*). The student with the answer card responds.

I HAVE: The magic fish created a storm and took away all of the wishes. *WHO HAS: Where did the fisherman and his wife live?	I HAVE: The wife wished for a larger cottage. WHO HAS: Was the wife happy with the larger cottage?
I HAVE: The fisherman and his wife lived in a hut by the sea. WHO HAS: What did the wife do all day?	I HAVE: No, the wife was not happy with the larger cottage. WHO HAS: What did the wife wish for next?
I HAVE: The wife took care of her garden of vegetables. WHO HAS: What was different about the fish the fisherman caught?	I HAVE: The wife wished for a castle. WHO HAS: Was the wife happy with the castle?
I HAVE: The fisherman caught a talking flounder. WHO HAS: What did the fish offer to do if the fisherman would let it go?	I HAVE: No, the wife was not happy with the castle. WHO HAS: What did the wife wish for next?
I HAVE: The fish offered to grant the fisherman and his wife a wish. WHO HAS: What did the wife wish for?	I HAVE: The wife wished to become queen and her husband an emperor. WHO HAS: What did the magic fish do?

The Fisherman and His Wife: Library Treasure Hunt

Go to the children's nonfiction shelves. Look for each number on the spine of the books. What is each book about? That is the missing word. Write it on the line after the number. The player who finds all of the missing words first is the winner.

1. The fisherman caught a magic 597. _____	2. The fisherman's wife worked in her 635. _____
3. The fisherman and his wife lived near the 551.46. _____	4. The wife wished for a 728.8. _____
5. The angry fish created a big 551.55. _____	6. This story is a 398.2. _____

Key: 1. fish; 2. garden; 3. ocean; 4. castle; 5. storm; 6. fairy tale

The Fisherman and His Wife: Word Search

E	M	P	E	R	O	R	C	W
N	A	M	R	E	H	S	I	F
E	K	A	A	D	E	F	W	C
G	I	F	H	N	E	T	A	U
A	N	M	H	U	S	S	I	E
T	G	M	R	O	T	S	S	A
T	O	R	E	L	E	T	O	R
O	O	K	E	F	T	E	E	R
C	G	R	M	I	A	S	A	E

Words to find:

fisherman	wife	flounder
cottage	castle	king
emperor	storm	hut

The Frog Prince

(The following can also be done orally, with the children raising their hands to respond.)

Find Someone Who!

Discover what your group has in common with the characters and places in *The Frog Prince.* Find a different name from the class or group for each item. The winner is the first to complete all eight items. The winner will then read each item and the person whose name is on each line will stand to verify that he or she can actually qualify for the item.

Find someone who . . .

1. Has lost a toy.   _____

2. Has had a frog for a pet.   _____

3. Can name one difference between a frog
   and a toad.   _____

4. Can name another story with a princess.   _____

5. Has kept a promise.   _____

6. Has walked in the woods.   _____

7. Has gotten water from a well.   _____

8. Has thrown something in anger.   _____

Storyteller's Introduction to *The Frog Prince*

After reading the following and before sharing the story or film, let the children give reasons for and against the frog allowing the princess to be his friend.

In the castle
Was a princess
Who had
A golden ball.
She tossed it high
Into the sky,
Then laughed
To watch it fall.
One day
she was upset
To see just
Where it fell.
Her golden ball
Had fallen
Into a deep
Dark well.
The princess
Cried and cried.
Her ball
Had disappeared.
Just then
At her side
A small green
frog appeared.
"Let me sit
At your table
And drink
from your cup
And eat
from your plate
and I'll bring
the ball up."

The princess
Nodded YES!
The frog retrieved
The ball.
The princess
Ran away.
Kept her promise?
NOT AT ALL!
That night
At the castle
The frog
Came to stay.
The princess
Was angry,
Told the frog
"GO AWAY!"
The king
Told the princess
That even if
She wept,
A promise
Is a promise.
A promise must
Be kept.
That night
In her room,
Beside herself
With rage,
The princess took
The frog
And threw him
In a cage.

But as the
Poor frog fell
Upon his
Prison floor,
The frog became
A prince.
He was a
Frog no more.
The princess
Told the prince
That they should
Become friends.
Do you think
He should say yes?
Now see how
This tale ends.

The Frog Prince: The Films

Duvall, Shelley, prod. 1982. *The Frog Prince.* Faerie Tale Theatre. Starring Teri Garr, Robin Williams. Live action color film. 60 minutes. Ages 10–adult. Several departures from the original tale, with some story lines not suitable for younger children. Distributed by Fox Video.

Golan-Globus Productions, prod. 1986. *The Frog Prince.* Starring Aileen Quinn, John Paragon, Helen Hunt. Live action color film. 86 minutes. Ages 6–adult. A musical adaptation with an extended story. Distributed by Cannon Video.

Halass and Batchelor, prod. 1969. *The Frog Prince.* Animated color film. 7 minutes. Ages 5–8. An accurate retelling of the original tale. Distributed by Britannica.

Henson, Jim, prod. 1988. *The Frog Prince.* Live action film with puppetry. 51 minutes. Ages 6–10. Using characters from *Sesame Street*, this film is enjoyable but quite different from the original tale. Distributed by Films, Inc.

Free viewing on the internet via YouTube: *The Frog Prince*, http://www.youtube .com/results?search_query=frog+prince+part+1&aq=4, running time 10:03.

The Frog Prince: The Books

Berenzy, Alix. 1991. *The Frog Prince.* New York: Henry Holt.

Crane, Walter. 2010. *The Frog Prince and Other Stories.* Minneapolis, MN: Filiquarian Classics.

Davidson, Susanna. 2008. *The Frog Prince.* Illustrated by Carl Gordon. London: Usborne.

Grimm, Jacob and Wilhelm. 2001. *The Frog Prince.* San Anselmo, CA: Treasure Bay.

Lothlorien, Elle. 2010. *The Frog Prince.* Seattle, WA: Amazon Digital Services.

Ormerod, Jan, illus. 2002. *The Frog Prince.* New York: Walker.

Porter, Jane. 2005. *The Frog Prince.* New York: Warner.

Ray, Jane, illus. 2000. "The Frog Prince," in *Fairy Tales Told by Berlie Doherty.* Somerville, MA: Candlewick Press.

Scieszka, Jon. 1991. *The Frog Prince Continued.* Illustrated by Steve Johnson. New York: Viking.

Stockham, Jessica. 2007. *The Frog Prince.* Flip-Up Fairy Tales. Swindon, Wiltshire, UK: Child's Play.

Tarcov, Edith H. 1993. *The Frog Prince.* Illustrated by James Marshall. New York: Cartwheel Books.

Wargin, Kathy-Jo. 2007. *The Frog Prince.* Illustrated by Anne Yvonne. Ann Arbor, MI: Mitten Press.

The Frog Prince: An Activity for Younger Children

Show books about Pond Life.
Play WHAT AM I?

What Am I?

(1)
WHO
Am I a frog or a hog?
WHERE
I can sit on a lily pad,
in the middle of a pond.
WHAT
I can leap high in the air
and catch flies for my dinner.
SO
I must be a _____.

(2)
WHO
Am I a tree or a bee?
WHERE
I am a queen.
I live in a hive filled with honey.
WHAT
My workers flit
from flower to flower
to bring me food.
SO
I must be a _____.

(3)
WHO
Am I a dish or a fish?
WHERE
My home is a pond
of clear blue water.
WHAT
I swim night and day and
catch small bugs on top of the water.
SO
I must be a _____.

(4)
WHO
Am I a fox or a box?
WHERE
My home is in the forest
near a clear blue pond.
WHAT
I drink from the pond in the early
morning being careful not to get
my bushy tail wet.
SO
I must be a _____.

Key: 1. frog; 2. bee; 3. fish; 4. fox

The Frog Prince: I HAVE, WHO HAS Game

Directions: Cut all the cards apart. Each player gets one card. Begin with the question preceded by an asterisk (*). The student with the answer card responds.

I HAVE: The prince and princess are married and live happily ever after. *WHO HAS: Where did the princess like to spend her time?	I HAVE: The frog asked to sit by her side and eat from her plate. WHO HAS: What happened when the princess agreed and the frog rescued the ball?
I HAVE: The princess spent her time in the woods by a cool well. WHO HAS: What was the favorite pastime of the princess?	I HAVE: The princess ran away and did not keep her promise. WHO HAS: What did the king do?
I HAVE: The princess spent her time throwing her golden ball and catching it. WHO HAS: How did the princess lose her ball?	I HAVE: The king insisted that the princess keep her promise. WHO HAS: What happened when the princess was alone with the frog in her room?
I HAVE: The ball rolled into the well. WHO HAS: Who offered to help retrieve the ball?	I HAVE: The angry princess threw the frog into a cage. WHO HAS: What happened when the frog hit the floor of the cage?
I HAVE: A frog offered to retrieve the ball. WHO HAS: What did the frog ask for in return?	I HAVE: The frog turned into a handsome prince. WHO HAS: How does the story end?

The Frog Prince: Library Treasure Hunt

Go to the children's nonfiction shelves. Look for each number on the spine of the books. What is each book about? That is the missing word. Write it on the line after the number. The player who finds all of the missing words first is the winner.

1. The princess lived in a 728.8. _____	2. She dropped her ball in the 363.6. _____
3. The ball was rescued by a 597.8. _____	4. A 133.4 had put a spell on a prince. _____
5. The frog wanted to be a 158 to the princess. _____	6. The princess did not have a loving 612.1. _____

Key: 1. castle; 2. water; 3. frog; 4. witch; 5. friend; 6. heart

The Frog Prince: Word Search

H	B	S	S	W	T	N	S
C	A	S	T	L	E	K	I
T	L	E	D	I	E	I	O
I	L	C	R	O	W	N	R
W	O	N	C	L	O	G	C
L	L	I	L	L	A	W	C
G	O	R	F	I	C	R	O
A	C	P	W	P	E	S	T

Words to find:

king	castle	woods
frog	ball	crown
princess	wall	witch

The Golden Goose

(The following can also be done orally, with the children raising their hands to respond.)

Find Someone Who!

Discover what your group has in common with the characters and places in *The Golden Goose*. Find a different name from the class or group for each item. The winner is the first to complete all eight items. The winner will then read each item and the person whose name is on each line will stand to verify that he or she can actually qualify for the item.

Find someone who . . .

1. Has two brothers.   _____

2. Has walked in a forest.   _____

3. Has shared lunch with someone.   _____

4. Is the youngest child in his or her family.   _____

5. Can make a sound like a goose.   _____

6. Can name a story with a princess.   _____

7. Has built a fire with sticks.   _____

8. Can name two words that rhyme with GOOSE.   _____

Storyteller's Introduction to *The Golden Goose*

Audience members respond with "THAT'S GOOD" or "THAT'S BAD" at a thumbs-up or thumbs-down signal from the storyteller.

Storyteller: A poor man had three sons and sent the oldest to the forest to chop wood to keep them warm when winter comes.

Audience: THAT'S GOOD.

Storyteller: No, that was bad, for the oldest son met a hungry dwarf in the woods and refused to share his food with him. He came home with almost no wood.

Audience: THAT'S BAD.

Storyteller: No, that was good, for it gave the second son a chance to go to the forest to chop wood to keep them warm when winter comes. He met the same hungry dwarf that his older brother met.

Audience: THAT'S GOOD.

Storyteller: It was bad because the second brother refused to share his food with the dwarf and went home with almost no wood to keep them warm when winter comes.

Audience: THAT'S BAD.

Storyteller: Not really, because it gave the youngest son a chance to go to the forest to chop wood to keep them warm when winter comes. There he met the same hungry dwarf and shared his food with him.

Audience: THAT'S GOOD.

Storyteller: In a way it was bad, for the dwarf was really a wizard and gave the boy a goose with golden feathers that lots of greedy people tried to steal.

Audience: THAT'S BAD.

Storyteller: It was really good, for as each greedy person became stuck to the goose it created a very funny sight, as the lad walked down the road carrying a goose with seven people stuck to it.

Audience: THAT'S GOOD.

Storyteller: Are you sure? Let's listen to the story *(or watch the film)* to decide if this funny sight was good or bad.

The Golden Goose: The Films

Duvall, Shelley, prod. 1984. *The Princess Who Had Never Laughed.* Faerie Tale Theatre. Starring Ellen Barkin, Howie Mandell, Howard Hesseman. Live action color film. 47 minutes. Ages 6–12. Varies considerably from the original Grimm tale. Distributed by Fox Video.

HBO Home Video, prod. 2000. *The Golden Goose.* Voices of B. D. Wong, Robert Pastorelli, Pam Grier, Ben Vereen, Samuel L. Jackson. Animated color film. 30 minutes. Ages 6–10. Follows the original tale closely. Available from Amazon.com.

Murray, K. Gordon, and Sheldon M. Schermer, prods. 2001. *The Golden Goose.* Starring Kaspar Eichel, Uwe Jessen, Peter Dommisch, Katharine Lind. Live action color film. 67 minutes. Ages 6–10. Varies from the original tale. Distributed by First Run Features.

Free viewing on the Internet via YouTube: *The Golden Goose,* http://www.youtube.com/watch?v=yDtRmrdo-NI, running time 7:33.

The Golden Goose: The Books

Angeletti, Roberta. 2010. *The Golden Goose.* Swindon, Wiltshire, UK: Child's Play.

Bradley, Kathleen. 2008. *The Goose That Laid the Golden Eggs.* Huntington Beach, CA: Teacher Created Materials.

Brooke, L. Leslie, illus. 1992. *The Golden Goose.* New York: Clarion.

Hillert, Margaret. 1950. *The Golden Goose.* Carlsbad, CA: Modern Curriculum Press.

Mackinnon, Mairi, Lesley Sims, and Daniel Howarth. 2006. *The Goose That Laid the Golden Eggs.* London: Usborne.

McDermott, Dennis. 2000. *The Golden Goose.* New York: Morrow Junior Books.

Shulevitz, Uri, illus. 1995. *The Golden Goose.* New York: Farrar.

Tulien, Sean. 2011. *The Golden Goose: A Grimm Graphic Novel.* Illustrated by Thiago Ferraz. Mankato, MN: Coughlan.

Watts, Bernadette. 2008. *The Golden Goose.* Japanese Edition. Houston, TX: Tsai Fong Books.

White, Mark. 2008. *The Goose That Laid the Golden Eggs: A Retelling of Aesop's Fable.* Mankato, MN: Coughlan Publishing.

The Golden Goose: Activities for Younger Children

Gather books about topics that begin with the letters G and P.

Example:

goats	pigs
gorillas	porcupines
gazelles	pandas
geese	parrots
geckos	peacocks

Tell the children you are going to sort the books into two piles. Topics that begin like goose go in the goose pile. Topics that begin like princess go in the princess pile. As you hold up each book, children will tell you in which pile the book belongs.

Play Look, See, Look.

_____

Look, See, Look

Leader: Look, see, look.
Find something in the room that begins with the letter P.
(Let children name as many items as they can.)

Leader: Look, see, look.
Find something in the room that begins with the letter G.
(Let children name as many items as they can.)

The Golden Goose: I HAVE, WHO HAS Game

Directions: Cut all the cards apart. Each player gets one card. Begin with the question preceded by an asterisk (*). The student with the answer card responds.

I HAVE: He offered the youngest brother his daughter's hand in marriage. *WHO HAS: What did the three brothers do for a living?	I HAVE: The innkeeper's three daughters tried to steal the goose. WHO HAS: Who else tried to steal the goose?
I HAVE: The three brothers chopped wood for a living. WHO HAS: Whom did the two older brothers meet in the forest?	I HAVE: A farmer, a miller, and two woodcutters tried to steal the goose. WHO HAS: What happened to each person who tried to steal the goose?
I HAVE: The two older brothers met a hungry dwarf in the forest. WHO HAS: What did the older brothers do when the dwarf asked for food?	I HAVE: Each person got stuck to the person before him or her. WHO HAS: Who laughed at the sight of the youngest brother trailed by seven people stuck to each other?
I HAVE: The older brothers refused to share their food with the dwarf. WHO HAS: What happened when the dwarf asked the youngest brother for food?	I HAVE: The princess laughed. WHO HAS: Why was the king surprised when the princess laughed?
I HAVE: Youngest brother shared his food and received a golden goose as a reward. WHO HAS: Who first tried to steal the goose?	I HAVE: It was the first time in her life that the princess had laughed. WHO HAS: What did the king offer the youngest brother?

The Golden Goose: Library Treasure Hunt

Go to the children's nonfiction shelves. Look for each number on the spine of the books. What is each book about? That is the missing word. Write it on the line after the number. The player who finds all of the missing words first is the winner.

1. Three brothers went to the 577.3 to chop wood for the winter. _____	2. Two brothers refused to share their 613.2 with a hungry dwarf. _____
3. The youngest son carried a goose to the king's 728.8. _____	4. A goose is a 598. _____
5. The goose's golden feathers glistened in the 525. _____	6. The princess gave her 612.1 to the youngest brother. _____

_____

Key: 1. forest; 2. food; 3. castle; 4. bird; 5. sun; 6. heart

The Golden Goose: Word Search

B	E	E	R	D	W	R	S
R	G	O	O	S	E	T	S
T	F	O	A	H	E	F	A
T	W	D	T	R	R	O	F
O	O	O	C	G	T	R	E
G	R	E	H	T	A	E	F
B	S	E	T	W	E	S	S
G	O	L	D	E	R	T	O

Words to find:

wood	forest	dwarf
brother	secret	tree
goose	gold	feather

Goldilocks and the Three Bears

(The following can also be done orally, with the children raising their hands to respond.)

Find Someone Who!

Discover what your group has in common with the characters and places in *Goldilocks and the Three Bears*. Find a different name from the class or group for each item. The winner is the first to complete all eight items. The winner will then read each item and the person whose name is on each line will stand to verify that he or she can actually qualify for the item.

Find someone who . . .

1. Has a name that begins with G.   _____

2. Has walked in the woods.   _____

3. Has seen a real bear.   _____

4. Likes hot oatmeal.   _____

5. Has broken something.   _____

6. Has a younger brother or sister.   _____

7. Has blonde hair.   _____

8. Knows what bears do in the winter.   _____

Storyteller's Introduction to *Goldilocks and the Three Bears*

At a signal from the storyteller, the children call out: "AND THEN . . ."

Storyteller:
Bowls of porridge
As a rule
Must be given
Time to cool.
Papa Bear said,
"Let's go out.
Let's go for
A walkabout."
Off they went,
Three bears together,
Bright blue sky,
Sunny weather.

Children:
AND THEN . . .

Storyteller:
A little girl
With golden hair
Found the house
With no one there.
Door was open,
Walked right in,
Spotted porridge
With a grin.

Children:
AND THEN . . .

Storyteller:
Ate the porridge,
Bowls were bare,
Then she saw
A little chair,
Painted red,
Made of oak,
Sat right down,
Small chair broke.

Children:
AND THEN . . .

Storyteller:
Went upstairs,
Sleepyhead,
Climbed into
A little bed.
Not expecting
A surprise,
Gave a yawn and
Closed her eyes.

Children:
AND THEN . . .

Storyteller:
Bears came home,
Bowls were bare,
In the parlor
Broken chair.
Going upstairs,
Wee Bear cried,
"Look! My bed
Is occupied!"
Will the child be
Foe or friend?
Hear the tale
To see the end.

Goldilocks and the Three Bears: The Films

Christianson Productions, prod. 1981. *Goldilocks and the Three Bears*. Animated color film. 10 minutes. Ages 3–6. Follows the original story line. Distributed by Phoenix/BFA Films and Video.

Duvall, Shelley, prod. 1983. *Goldilocks and the Three Bears*. Faerie Tale Theatre. Starring Tatum O'Neal, John Lithgow, Hoyt Axton. Live action color film. 60 minutes. Ages 3–8. An enjoyable film but varies considerably from the original tale. Released on DVD 2004. Distributed by Fox Video.

Field, David, and Roddy Lee, prods. 1995. *Goldilocks and the Three Bears*. Delta Animated Film Classics Series. Animated color film. 50 minutes. Ages 3–6. Follows the original tale with some additions. Available from Amazon.com or Barnes&Noble.com.

Phoenix Learning Group, prod. 2008. *Goldilocks and the Three Bears*. Animated color film. 12 minutes. Ages 3–6. Faithfully follows the original tale. A Coronet release. Available from Amazon.com.

Free viewing on the Internet via YouTube: *Goldilocks and the Three Bears*, http://www .youtube.com/watch?v=Oaw-d3r_gIc, running time 2:30; musical version at http://www .youtube.com/watch?v=UaulRHrJGeU, running time 5:53.

Goldilocks and the Three Bears: The Books

Aylesworth, Jim. 2003. *Goldilocks and the Three Bears*. Illustrated by Barbara McClintock. New York: Scholastic.

Brooke, L. Leslie. 2011. *The Three Bears*. South Sioux City, ME: A. J. Publishing.

Buehner, Caralyn, and Mark Buehner. 2000. *Goldilocks and the Three Bears*. New York: Dial Books for Young Readers.

Child, Lauren. 2009. *Goldilocks and the Three Bears*. Photography by Polly Borland. New York: Disney-Hyperion Books.

Clark, Emma Chichester. 2010. *Goldilocks and the Three Bears*. Somerville, MA: Candlewick.

Galdone, Paul. 2011. *The Three Bears*. New York: HMH.

Hefferan, Rob. 2003. *Three Bears*. New York: Random House.

Hillert, Margaret. 2006. *The Three Bears*. Illustrated by Irma Wilde. Chicago: Norwood House Press.

Kurtz, John, illus. 2004. *Goldilocks and the Three Bears*. New York: Jump at the Sun/ Hyperion Books for Children.

Lively, Penelope. 2004. *Goldilocks and the Three Bears*. Illustrated by Debi Gliori. London: Hodder Children's.

Marshall, James. 1998. *Goldilocks and the Three Bears*. New York: Dial.

Piumini, Roberto. 2010. *Goldilocks and the Three Bears*. Illustrated by Valentina Salmaso. Mankato, MN: Picture Window Books.

Sanderson, Ruth. 2009. *Goldilocks*. New York: Little, Brown and Company.

Spirin, Gennady. 2009. *Goldilocks and the Three Bears*. Tarrytown, NY: Marshall Cavendish.

Stanley, Diane. 2003. *Goldie and the Three Bears*. New York: HarperCollins.

Wade, Barrie. 2003. *Goldilocks and the Three Bears*. Illustrated by Kristina Stephenson. Mankato, MN: Picture Window Books.

Goldilocks and the Three Bears: Activities for Younger Children

Display books about forest animals.

Leader: Goldilocks took a walk in the forest. Here are books about animals she might have seen.

Hold up the books one at a time. Recite the lines by adding the name of the animal the book is about.

Examples:

> Walking through the forest what do I see?
> I see a <u>bear</u> looking at me.

> Walking through the forest what do I see?
> I see a <u>rabbit</u> looking at me.

> Walking through the forest what do I see?
> I see a <u>fox</u> looking at me.

> Walking through the forest what do I see?
> I see a <u>deer</u> looking at me.

> Walking through the forest what do I see?
> I see a <u>squirrel</u> looking at me.

> Walking through the forest what do I see?
> I see a <u>turtle</u> looking at me.

> Walking through the forest what do I see?
> I see a <u>raccoon</u> looking at me.

A Three Bears Counting Rhyme

Display picture books about different types of bears.
(Children call out the missing number.)

> Five brown bears walking out the door
> One stayed behind and then there were _____. *(four)*
>
> Four panda bears sitting in a tree
> One fell down and then there were _____. *(three)*
>
> Three grizzly bears look how big they grew
> One took a nap and then there were _____. *(two)*
>
> Two baby bears playing in the sun
> Both ran away and then there were _____. *(none)*

A Three Bears Song

(Tune: "London Bridge")

> Goldilocks went for a walk, for a walk, for a walk.
> Goldilocks went for a walk,
> Found a cottage.
>
> Found some porridge, ate it up, ate it up, ate it up.
> Found some porridge, ate it up,
> She was hungry.
>
> Sat right down and broke a chair, broke a chair, broke a chair.
> Sat right down and broke a chair,
> All to pieces.
>
> Went upstairs and crawled in bed, crawled in bed, crawled in bed.
> Went upstairs and crawled in bed,
> She was sleepy.
>
> What will happen when bears come home, bears come home, bears come home?
> What will happen when bears come home?
> Read the story.

Goldilocks and the Three Bears: I HAVE, WHO HAS Game

Directions: Cut all the cards apart. Each player gets one card. Begin with the question preceded by an asterisk (*). The student with the answer card responds.

I HAVE: Goldilocks woke up and ran home. *WHO HAS: Why did the bears go for a walk?	I HAVE: She went to sleep in Wee Bear's bed. WHO HAS: What happened when the three bears came home?
I HAVE: The bears went for a walk to let their porridge cool. WHO HAS: Who arrived at the bears' house?	I HAVE: They saw someone had eaten their porridge. WHO HAS: What did the bears find in the parlor?
I HAVE: Goldilocks arrived at the bears' house. WHO HAS: What did Goldilocks do in the kitchen?	I HAVE: In the parlor they found Wee Bear's broken chair. WHO HAS: What did the three bears find upstairs?
I HAVE: Goldilocks ate the porridge. WHO HAS: What did Goldilocks do in the parlor?	I HAVE: Upstairs they found two beds mussed up. WHO HAS: What did the bears find in Wee Bear's bed?
I HAVE: Goldilocks sat in Wee Bear's chair and broke it. WHO HAS: What did Goldilocks do upstairs?	I HAVE: The bears found Goldilocks asleep in Wee Bear's bed. WHO HAS: What did Goldilocks do?

Goldilocks and the Three Bears: Library Treasure Hunt

Go to the children's nonfiction shelves. Look for each number on the spine of the books. What is each book about? That is the missing word. Write it on the line after the number. The player who finds all of the missing words first is the winner.

1. The animals in this story are 599.78. _____	2. Goldilocks found a 690 in the woods. _____
3. The bears went for a walk in the 577.3. _____	4. Breaking and entering is against the 328. _____
5. The bears walked among the 582.16. _____	6. A mother, father, and child are all part of a 306.8. _____

Key: 1. bears; 2. house; 3. forest; 4. law; 5. trees; 6. family

Goldilocks and the Three Bears: Word Search

A	G	O	R	G	A	D	A	C	E
A	C	B	H	S	E	S	W	O	T
L	L	E	A	C	C	L	E	D	D
S	P	D	G	I	L	W	E	D	R
A	A	A	I	D	R	R	B	C	P
F	B	E	P	B	I	B	E	M	W
E	M	A	M	A	G	R	A	G	R
O	O	C	H	T	S	E	R	O	F
S	K	C	O	L	I	D	L	O	G
R	L	L	P	I	O	O	R	E	P

Words to find:

Wee Bear	mama	papa
porridge	chair	bed
girl	Goldilocks	forest

The Goose Girl

(The following can also be done orally, with the children raising their hands to respond.)

Find Someone Who!

Discover what your group has in common with the characters and places in *The Goose Girl*. Find a different name from the class or group for each item. The winner is the first to complete all eight items. The winner will then read each item and the person whose name is on each line will stand to verify that he or she can actually qualify for the item.

Find someone who . . .

1. Has traveled more than 5 miles from home.   _____

2. Has seen a real goose.   _____

3. Can name an evil fairy tale character.   _____

4. Has lost a handkerchief.   _____

5. Has waded in a stream.   _____

6. Has worn a disguise.   _____

7. Can name a fairy tale with a prince.   _____

8. Can name another fairy tale.   _____

Storyteller's Introduction to *The Goose Girl*

Let the audience practice this verse, which they will recite at a signal from the storyteller:

If her mother only knew,
Her heart would surely break in two.

Storyteller:
A prince had asked
For the princess's hand
To become his bride
In a far off land.
She set out with her maid
And a carriage of course,
A magic silk hankie,
And her talking horse.
The queen sent the hankie,
A magical charm,
To keep the sweet princess
From coming to harm,
But approaching a stream
That had to be crossed,
She bent down to drink
And the hankie was lost.

Audience:
If her mother only knew,
Her heart would surely break in two.

Storyteller:
Now, of the two women,
The maid was the stronger,
Took the place of the princess,
Would serve her no longer.
They arrived in the kingdom,
Not recognized since

The two had changed places,
Deceiving the prince.
The maid killed the horse
So its talking would cease,
Set the princess to work,
Looking after the geese.

Audience:
If her mother only knew,
Her heart would surely break in two.

Storyteller:
Conrad, the goose herd,
Worked at her side
And soon told the king
She had something to hide.
The king asked the goose girl
To tell him her tale
And said he would see
That right would prevail.
Now do you suppose
He sent for the maid
To punish the girl
For the switch she had made?
Did the maid and the princess
Become best of friends?
Read the book,
Watch the film,
To see how it ends.

The Goose Girl: The Films

Genschow, Fritz, prod. 1967. *The Goose Girl.* Starring Fritz Genschow, Gunter Hertel, Renee Stobrawa. Live action color film. 78 minutes. Ages 6–12. Faithful to the original story. Available from Amazon.com.

Davenport, Tom, and Mimi Davenport, prods. 1984. *The Goose Girl.* Live action color film. 18 minutes. Ages 5–10. Follows the original tale closely. Distributed by Davenport Films.

Institut für Film und Bild, prod. 1990. *The Goosemaid.* Color film with very limited animation. 10 minutes. Ages 5–8. Follows the original story line. Distributed by Britannica.

The Goose Girl: The Books

Cross, Gillian. 1998. *The Goose Girl.* Illustrated by Helen Cooper. New York: Scholastic.

DeAngeli, Marguerite. 1964. *The Goose Girl.* New York: Doubleday.

The Goose Girl. 1982. Well-Loved Tales. Ladybird Series. New York: Penguin.

Kimmel, Eric. 1995. *The Goose Girl.* Illustrated by Rob Sauber. New York: Holiday House, 1995.

Lang, Andrew, ed. 1965. "The Goose Girl," in *The Blue Fairy Book.* Illustrated by H. J. Ford and G. P. Jacob Hood. Mineola, NY: Dover.

Linklater, Eric. 1992. *The Goose Girl and Other Stories.* North Pomfret, VT: Trafalgar Square.

Lintern, A. W. 1952. *The Goose-Girl: A Play in Three Acts.* London: Pitman.

McLellan, Joe, Matrine McLellan, and Joseph McLellan. 2006. *The Goose Girl.* Winnipeg: Pemmican.

Woodhead, Constance. 1952. *The Little Goose-Girl.* Sunbeam Stories Series. New York: Warne.

The Goose Girl: A Song for Younger Children

An Animal Song

(Tune: "Skip to My Lou")

(Choose an animal.

Name two things it has.

Name two things it eats.

Name one thing it does.)

(Has) A great grey goose has <u>feathers and a beak</u>.

(Has) A great grey goose has <u>feathers and a beak</u>.

(Eats) A great gray goose eats <u>corn and bugs</u>,

(Does) And <u>flies in the sky</u>.

(Choose a different animal.

Fill in the blank spaces.

Sing the song.)

(Has) A _____ has _____ and _____.

(Has) A _____ has _____ and _____.

(Eats) A _____ eats _____ and _____,

(Does) And _____.

The Goose Girl: I HAVE, WHO HAS Game

Directions: Cut all the cards apart. Each player gets one card. Begin with the question preceded by an asterisk (*). The student with the answer card responds.

I HAVE: He revealed the real princess to the prince and punished the maid. *WHO HAS: Why was the princess traveling to a far-off land?	I HAVE: The maid forced the princess to change places with her. WHO HAS: What did the maid do to the horse?
I HAVE: She was going to a far-off land to marry a prince. WHO HAS: What did the princess take with her?	I HAVE: The maid killed the horse. WHO HAS: What happened to the princess when they reached the far-off kingdom?
I HAVE: She took wedding clothes, a talking horse, and her maid. WHO HAS: What did her mother give her for the journey?	I HAVE: The princess was forced to look after the geese. WHO HAS: Who accused the princess of causing strange things to happen?
I HAVE: Her mother gave her a magic hankie to keep her from harm. WHO HAS: What happened to the hankie?	I HAVE: The gooseherd told the king of the strange things that happen around the goose girl. WHO HAS: What did the king do?
I HAVE: The hankie fell into a stream and was swept away. WHO HAS: What did the maid do?	I HAVE: He listened while the goose girl told her tale to an iron stove. WHO HAS: What did the king do after hearing the tale?

The Goose Girl: Library Treasure Hunt

Go to the children's nonfiction shelves. Look for each number on the spine of the books. What is each book about? That is the missing word. Write it on the line after the number. The player who finds all of the missing words first is the winner.

1. The princess had a talking 636.1. _____	2. The princess told the maid to fetch some 363.6. _____
3. The princess traveled to a 728.8 in a far-off land. _____	4. The princess lost her magic hankie in a 577.6. _____
5. The princess took with her some wedding 391. _____	6. This story is a 398.2. _____

Key: 1. horse; 2. water; 3. castle; 4. river; 5. clothing; 6. fairy tale

The Goose Girl: Word Search

O	R	M	A	I	D	E	E
H	E	A	R	T	R	S	O
A	T	G	T	O	O	K	L
H	A	O	E	O	N	C	E
O	W	B	G	I	R	O	E
R	G	L	F	S	E	E	E
S	S	E	C	N	I	R	P
E	L	T	S	A	C	T	R

Words to find:

maid	horse	knife
water	goblet	heart
goose	castle	princess

Hansel and Gretel

(The following can also be done orally, with the children raising their hands to respond.)

Find Someone Who!

Discover what your group has in common with the characters and places in *Hansel and Gretel*. Find a different name from the class or group for each item. The winner is the first to complete all eight items. The winner will then read each item and the person whose name is on each line will stand to verify that he or she can actually qualify for the item.

Find someone who . . .

1. Has one brother.   _____

2. Has one sister.   _____

3. Has been lost in the woods.   _____

4. Has made a gingerbread house at
   Christmastime.   _____

5. Can name another story with a witch.   _____

6. Has given food to a hungry person.   _____

7. Has a first name that begins with H.   _____

8. Has a first name that begins with G.   _____

Storyteller's Introduction to *Hansel and Gretel*

At a signal from the storyteller, the children respond "OH, NO!" when the right hand is raised and "OH, YES!" when the left hand is raised.

Storyteller:	**Audience:**
Once upon a time a family of four	
Had very little food because they were so poor.	
The wife said to the father, "Take the children to the wood.	
Leave them in the forest so we're rid of them for good."	OH, NO!
"Oh, no," the father said, "Suppose a wild beast,	
Should find my darling children and eat them piece by piece?"	
"We have no choice," the wife said. "We are desperate and in need.	
When you leave them in the forest that is two less mouths to feed."	OH, NO!
But Hansel heard the wife tell what feeding them would cost,	
So he came up with a plan to keep from getting lost.	
The father led the way through the forest up ahead.	
Hansel marked the path they trod with pieces of his bread.	OH, YES!
But hungry birds were following. They ate up every bite.	
The children could not find their home in the darkness of the night.	OH, NO!
When morning came they found a house a glistening sugar treat	
Made of candy, bread and cakes so they began to eat.	
They heard a sound and saw an old woman at the door	
"Come in, dear ones," she told the two,"Come in and have some more."	OH, YES!
But when the two had entered she flew into a rage	
Ordered Gretel to fetch water, put Hansel in a cage.	
For she planned to cook both children whether fattened up or not	
Piled up sticks to make a fire to get the oven hot.	OH, NO!
The witch then ordered Gretel to quickly crawl inside	
To test the oven temperature "Show me," the girl replied.	
The witch then stuck her head in, Gretel pushed her with a jolt	
Making sure she was inside, slammed the door and shot the bolt.	OH, YES!
Back into the forest we see the children roam	
But soon they both discover the path that leads them home.	
The stepmother is gone and father sheds his tears of joy	
His dear children have come home his little girl and boy.	
The father got a job doing that for which he's able	
So now there's food a plenty on the little cottage table.	OH, YES!

Hansel and Gretel: The Films

Austin, Steven, and Jonathan Bogner, prods. 2003. *Hansel and Gretel.* Warner Brothers film. Starring Jacob Smith, Taylor Momsen, Dakota Fanning, Lynn Redgrave, Howie Mandel. Live action color film. 89 minutes. Ages 6–12. Departs considerably from the original tale with the addition of a sandman, a fairy, and a troll. Distributed by Innovation Film Group.

Duvall, Shelley, prod. 1982. *Hansel and Gretel.* Faerie Tale Theatre. Starring Ricky Schroeder, Joan Collins, Paul Dooley, Bridgette Anderson. Live action color film. 51 minutes. Ages 7–12. Follows the original tale closely but more suitable for older children. Distributed by Fox Video.

Golam, Menahem, Patricia Ruben, and Itzik Kol, prods. 2005. *Hansel and Gretel.* Cannon Movie Tales Series. Starring David Warner, Hugh Pollard, Nicola Stapleton, Emily Richard, Cloris Leachman. Live action color film. 84 minutes. Ages 5–12. Faithful to the original with addition of a few characters and musical numbers. Distributed by MGM Video. Available from Amazon.com and Barnes&Noble.com.

Good Times Video, prod. 2006. *Hansel and Gretel.* Timeless Tales Series. Animated color film. 50 minutes. Ages 4–8. Faithful rendition of the original tale. Distributed by Gaiam Americas Studio. Available from Amazon.com and Barnes&Noble.com.

Free viewing on the Internet via YouTube and Hulu: *Hansel and Gretel,* http://www.youtube.com/movie?v=oexVytEUMEg&ob=av1n&feature=mv_sr, running time 1:13:22, and http://www.hulu.com/watch/112374/shelley-duvalls-faerie-tale-theatre-hansel-and-gretel, running time 48:40.

Hansel and Gretel: The Books

Abeyà, Elisabet. 2005. *Hansel and Gretel.* Illustrated by Cristina Losant. San Francisco: Chronicle Books.

Archipova, Anastasiya. 2008. *Hansel and Gretel.* Edinburgh, UK: Floris.

Brooke, Samantha. 2009. *Hansel and Gretel.* New York: Penguin.

Brothers Grimm. 2001. *Hansel and Gretel.* Illustrated by Dorothée Duntze. New York: North-South Books.

Crawford, Elizabeth D. 2008. *Hansel and Gretel.* Illustrated by Lisbeth Zwerger. New York: Penguin Group.

Galdone, Paul. 1982. *Hansel and Gretel.* New York: McGraw Hill.

Isadora, Rachel. 2009. *Hansel and Gretel.* New York: G. P. Putnam's Sons.

Lesser, Rika. 1999. *Hansel and Gretel.* Illustrated by Paul O. Zelinsky. New York: Putnam.

Mayer, Mercer. 2010. *Hansel and Gretel: A Lift-the-Flap Book.* Little Critter Series. New York: Sterling.

Moses, Will. 2006. *Hansel and Gretel.* New York: Philomel.

Petrlik, Andrea, illus. 2009. *Hansel and Gretel.* New York: Penguin.

Piumini, Roberto. 2010. *Hansel and Gretel.* Illustrated by Anna Laura Cantone. Mankato, MN: Picture Window Books.

Price, Margaret Evans. 2005. *Hansel and Gretel.* Seattle: Laughing Elephant.

Rylant, Cynthia. 2008. *Hansel and Gretel.* Illustrated by Jen Corace. New York: Hyperion Books for Children.

Hansel and Gretel: A Song for Younger Children

A Hansel and Gretel Song

(Tune: "Have You Ever Seen a Lassie?")

If I met a wicked witch,
A wicked witch,
A wicked witch,
If I met a wicked witch,
I would look like this.

(Children show how they would look.)

If I got lost in the woods,
In the woods,
In the woods,
If I got lost in the woods,
I would look like this.

(Children show how they would look.)

If I found a candy house,
A candy house,
A candy house,
If I found a candy house,
I would look like this.

(Children show how they would look.)

If my pa said, "Welcome home,
Welcome home,
Welcome home,"
If my pa said, "Welcome home,"
I would look like this.

(Children show how they would look.)

Hansel and Gretel: I HAVE, WHO HAS Game

Directions: Cut all the cards apart. Each player gets one card. Begin with the question preceded by an asterisk (*). The student with the answer card responds.

I HAVE: Precious jewels. *WHO HAS: What was the problem with the family of Hansel and Gretel?	I HAVE: The wild birds ate the bread crumbs. WHO HAS: What did the children find in the woods?
I HAVE: The family was very poor with not enough to eat. WHO HAS: What did the stepmother propose?	I HAVE: The children found a house made of bread, cake, and candy. WHO HAS: What did the children do to the house?
I HAVE: The stepmother wanted to take the children into the woods and leave them. WHO HAS: How did the father feel about the stepmother's plan?	I HAVE: The hungry children began to eat the house. WHO HAS: Who did the house belong to?
I HAVE: The father objected to the plan but finally went along with it. WHO HAS: How did Hansel plan to get back home?	I HAVE: The house belonged to a witch who planned to eat Hansel. WHO HAS: How did the children escape?
I HAVE: Hansel planned to follow a trail of bread crumbs home. WHO HAS: What happened to the bread crumbs?	I HAVE: Gretel pushed the witch into the oven. WHO HAS: What riches did the children find and take home?

Hansel and Gretel: Library Treasure Hunt

Go to the children's nonfiction shelves. Look for each number on the spine of the books. What is each book about? That is the missing word. Write it on the line after the number. The player who finds all of the missing words first is the winner.

1. Hansel and Gretel's father did not have any 332.4. _____	2. The children were led deep into the 577.3. _____
3. A 598 ate the bread crumbs Hansel dropped. _____	4. The children went to sleep under the 582.16. _____
5. The gingerbread house was owned by a 133.4. _____	6. They brought 745.58 home. _____

Key: 1. money; 2. forest; 3. bird; 4. trees; 5. witch; 6. jewels

Hansel and Gretel: Word Search

S	S	A	H	C	D	L	H	R
E	B	F	N	F	S	S	C	F
U	M	A	A	T	J	F	U	E
G	U	T	W	H	C	T	I	W
E	R	H	C	A	N	D	Y	F
O	C	E	B	N	L	I	Y	E
W	V	R	T	S	E	R	O	F
R	J	E	W	E	L	S	W	T
W	A	O	N	L	L	L	R	S

Words to find:

Hansel	Gretel	father
forest	crumbs	witch
candy	oven	jewels

The Happy Prince

(The following can also be done orally, with the children raising their hands to respond.)

Find Someone Who!

Discover what your group has in common with the characters and places in *The Happy Prince*. Find a different name from the class or group for each item. The winner is the first to complete all eight items. The winner will then read each item and the person whose name is on each line will stand to verify that he or she can actually qualify for the item.

Find someone who . . .

1. Has collected cans of food for needy people. _____

2. Has donated clothing to charity. _____

3. Has seen a statue in a town square. _____

4. Can name three different kinds of birds. _____

5. Can name something made of gold. _____

6. Can name two different precious stones. _____

7. Knows what color a ruby is. _____

8. Can name another story with a prince. _____

Storyteller's Introduction to *The Happy Prince*

In the center of a village stood the statue of a prince.
Once a happy fellow, he had passed away and since
The people wished to honor him, they made a plan so bold
To give him eyes of sapphires and a cloak with leaves of gold.

Now a swallow saw the statue, said, "I'll make my home right here."
He tucked his head beneath his wing and then he felt a tear.
The Happy Prince was crying, he saw misery all around.
Hunger, cold, and poverty were sad sights to be found.

The prince spoke to the swallow, as he heard the children's cries,
"Take the gold leaves from my cloak, take the sapphires from my eyes,
Give them to the needy, to the hungry, to the poor.
I have no need for sapphires. Gold leaves I need no more."

When the villagers awoke and saw the statue standing there,
"Look! Just look!" they cried aloud, "Our statue is all bare!
It's not handsome, it is ugly, we don't want it in our town.
Take the statue to the furnace and proceed to melt it down."

So the statue in small pieces was melted part by part,
But the one thing that would not melt was the prince's broken heart.

When the Lord sent all his angels a most precious thing to find,
In the village where the people proved themselves to be unkind,
The angels searched the village, yes, the angels looked around.
Can you guess the thing, the only thing, the thing the angels found?

(Let the children guess.)

The good Lord smiled and said to them, "The choice you made was wise.
The Happy Prince shall smile again with ME in paradise."

The Happy Prince: The Films

Potterton Productions, prod. 1974. *The Happy Prince.* Voices of Christopher Plummer, Glynis Johns, John Codner, Jill Frappier, Howard Ryshpan. Animated color film. 25 minutes. Ages 6–12. An excellent film that follows the original story line. Distributed by Pyramid Film and Video. Available from Amazon.com and Barnes&Noble.com.

Romania Films, prod. 1981. *The Happy Prince.* Animated color film. 8 minutes. Ages 6–10. A shortened version of the original tale. Distributed by Phoenix/BFA Films and Video.

Free viewing on the Internet via YouTube: *The Happy Prince*, http://www.youtube.com/watch?v=Ixd9gPjiN4s, running time 10:05, ages 7–12.

The Happy Prince: The Books

Grodrin, Elissa. 2005. *The Happy Prince.* Chelsea, MI: Sleeping Bear Press.

Wilde, Oscar. 1983. *The Happy Prince.* Piccolo Picture Books. London: Pan Books.

Wilde, Oscar. 1989. *The Happy Prince.* Illustrated by Ed Young. New York: Simon and Schuster.

Wilde, Oscar. 1994. *The Happy Prince.* Illustrated by Jane Ray. New York: Dutton.

Wilde, Oscar. 2000. *The Happy Prince and Other Stories.* Chestnut Hill, MA: Adamant Media.

Wilde, Oscar. 2006. *The Happy Prince and Other Tales.* West Valley City, UT: Walking Lion Press.

Wilde, Oscar. 2009. *The Happy Prince and Other Stories.* Illustrated by Lars Bo. New York: Puffin.

Wilde, Oscar. 2010. *The Happy Prince and Other Tales.* Illustrated by Charles Robinson. London: Smart Bookworms.

Wilde, Oscar, and Harriet Golden. 2001. *The Happy Prince and Other Fairy Tales.* Mineola, NY: Dover.

Wilde, Oscar, and George Percy. 2010. *The Happy Prince: And Other Tales.* Charleston, SC: Nabu.

Zipes, Jack, illus. 2008. *Complete Fairy Tales of Oscar Wilde.* New York: Signet Classics.

The Happy Prince: I HAVE, WHO HAS Game

Directions: Cut all the cards apart. Each player gets one card. Begin with the question preceded by an asterisk (*). The student with the answer card responds.

I HAVE: It was taken to Heaven by the angels. *WHO HAS: Why did the Town Councillors decide to build a statue of the prince?	I HAVE: The statue cried because of the misery he saw all around him. WHO HAS: What was the first thing the prince told the swallow to do?
I HAVE: The prince was happy in life so the Councillors wanted a happy statue. WHO HAS: What was special about the statue of the Happy Prince?	I HAVE: The prince said to take a ruby from its sword and give it to a poor mother and child for food. WHO HAS: What else did the prince give away?
I HAVE: The statue had sapphires for eyes, rubies on its sword, and leaves of gold for its cloak. WHO HAS: What creature decided to make the statue its home?	I HAVE: The prince gave sapphires to a freezing man and a match girl. WHO HAS: How did the swallow help the blind prince?
I HAVE: A little swallow went to sleep on the statue's feet. WHO HAS: Why did the swallow feel drops of water on its wings?	I HAVE: The swallow told the prince of other needs until the prince gave away all of his gold leaves. WHO HAS: What did the people of the town do to the bare statue?
I HAVE: The swallow felt drops of water because the statue was crying. WHO HAS: Why was the statue of the prince crying?	I HAVE: The people melted the statue, but its heart did not melt. WHO HAS: What happened to the prince's heart?

The Happy Prince: Library Treasure Hunt

Go to the children's nonfiction shelves. Look for each number on the spine of the books. What is each book about? That is the missing word. Write it on the line after the number. The player who finds all of the missing words first is the winner.

1. A small 598 slept at the foot of the statue. _____	2. The statue of the Happy Prince had 745.58 for eyes. _____
3. People who live in poverty have little or no 332.4. _____	4. The 391 on the statue was covered with gold leaves. _____
5. All of the statue melted except for its 612.1. _____	6. 296.1 took the Happy Prince's heart to paradise. _____

Key: 1. bird; 2. jewels; 3. money; 4. clothing; 5. heart; 6. Angels

The Happy Prince: Word Search

E	C	N	I	R	P	W	R	U
E	S	Y	D	Y	E	S	E	L
H	W	L	N	A	R	B	G	I
W	O	L	L	A	W	S	N	H
G	R	G	E	E	T	L	U	V
Y	D	T	N	A	O	E	H	W
C	B	A	T	S	V	V	S	C
E	S	U	L	U	S	E	R	L
S	E	V	R	A	D	S	S	S

Words to find:

prince	statue	swallow
leaves	gold	sword
ruby	hunger	tears

How the Camel Got His Hump

(By Rudyard Kipling)

(The following can also be done orally, with the children raising their hands to respond.)

Find Someone Who!

Discover what your group has in common with the characters and places in *How the Camel Got His Hump*. Find a different name from the class or group for each item. The winner is the first to complete all eight items. The winner will then read each item and the person whose name is on each line will stand to verify that he or she can actually qualify for the item.

Find someone who . . .

1. Can name something a camel eats.　　_____

2. Can give the name of one desert.　　_____

3. Has ridden a horse.　　_____

4. Has a dog for a pet.　　_____

5. Can say a word that rhymes with OX.　　_____

6. Has done someone else's work.　　_____

7. Has gone one day without eating.　　_____

8. Can name the author of the *Just So Stories*.　　_____

Storyteller's Introduction to *How the Camel Got His Hump*

Each time the storyteller raises a hand, the audience members will give a loud "HUMPH!"

Long, long ago when the world was new
And animals worked for man,
They fetched and they carried, they ploughed and they scrubbed,
And they made the world quite spic and span,
Except for a camel, asked to help by the horse,
Replied with a loud "HUMPH!" of course.

The dog came along with a stick in its mouth,
He worked with the ox and the horse,
But the camel was lazy and when asked to help
Replied with a loud "HUMPH!" of course.

The ox with his yoke ploughed the field for the man,
With the help of the dog and the horse,
But the camel when asked to plough like the rest
Replied with a loud "HUMPH!" of course.

So the dog and the horse and the ox worked away,
Three were doing the work of four,
They told the camel that this wasn't fair
But the camel said "HUMPH!" once more.

Then a man who made magic looked at the beast
And caused a great hump to rise,
On the back of the camel it grew and grew
And gave the beast quite a surprise.

So the camel's hump is an ugly lump
Which well you may see at the zoo,
But uglier yet is the hump we get
From having too little to do.

How the Camel Got His Hump: The Films

Coronet, prod. 1984. *How the Camel Got His Hump.* Limited animation color film. 11 minutes. Ages 5–8. Adaptation faithful to the original tale. Distributed by Coronet/MTI Film and Video.

Graber, Sheila, prod. 1998. *Rudyard Kipling's Just So Stories: Volume 1.* Animated full-color film. 53 minutes. Ages 5–8. Contains, among other tales, "How the Camel Got His Hump." Available from Amazon.com.

Free viewing on the Internet via YouTube: *How the Camel Got His Hump,* http://www.youtube.com/watch?v=4afoxwg-BH0.

How the Camel Got His Hump: The Books

Fontes, Justine, and Ron Fontes. 2001. *How the Camel Got Its Hump.* Illustrated by Keiko Motoyama. New York: Golden Books.

Jones, Christianne C. 2005. *How the Camel Got Its Hump.* Illustrated by Ronnie Rooney. Mankato, MN: Picture Window Books.

Kipling, Rudyard. 1996. *Just So Stories.* Illustrated by Barry Moser. New York: Morrow.

Kipling, Rudyard. 2001. *How the Camel Got Its Hump.* Illustrated by Lisbeth Zwerger. New York: North-South Books.

Kipling, Rudyard. 2001. *Just So Stories.* Mineola, NY: Dover.

Kipling, Rudyard. 2009. *Just So Stories.* Edison, NJ: Chartwell Books.

Lewis, Lisa. 2009. *Just So Stories: For Little Children.* New York: Oxford University Press.

Lisle, Janet Taylor. 2002. *Just So Stories.* New York: Simon and Schuster.

Stroud, Jonathan. 2008. *Just So Stories.* New York: Penguin.

How the Camel Got His Hump: I HAVE, WHO HAS Game

Directions: Cut all the cards apart. Each player gets one card. Begin with the question preceded by an asterisk (*). The student with the answer card responds.

I HAVE: The hump stored food so the camel could work three days without eating. *WHO HAS: Where did the camel in this story live?	I HAVE: The dog asked the camel to fetch and carry. WHO HAS: How did the camel respond to the dog?
I HAVE: The camel lived in the middle of a desert. WHO HAS: What did the camel say when spoken to?	I HAVE: The camel said "Humph" to the dog. WHO HAS: What did the camel say when the ox asked the camel to plough?
I HAVE: When spoken to, the camel said, "Humph." WHO HAS: What did the horse ask the camel to do?	I HAVE: The camel said "Humph" to the ox. WHO HAS: What did the angry horse, dog, and ox do?
I HAVE: The horse asked the camel to come out and trot. WHO HAS: Why did the camel say "Humph" to the horse?	I HAVE: They held a pow-wow and told the Djinn about the lazy camel. WHO HAS: What did the Djinn do when the camel refused to work?
I HAVE: The camel was lazy and did not want to work. WHO HAS: What did the dog ask the camel to do?	I HAVE: The Djinn gave the camel a hump. WHO HAS: How was the hump useful to the camel?

How the Camel Got His Hump: Library Treasure Hunt

Go to the children's nonfiction shelves. Look for each number on the spine of the books. What is each book about? That is the missing word. Write it on the line after the number. The player who finds all of the missing words first is the winner.

1. The camel lived in a 577.5. _____	2. The 636.1 asked the camel to trot. _____
3. The 636.7 asked the camel to fetch and carry. _____	4. The 637 asked the camel to help plough. _____
5. The Djinn began to work great 973.8. _____	6. This story is about a lazy 599.63. _____

Key: 1. desert; 2. horse; 3. dog; 4. ox (cattle); 5. magic; 6. camel

How the Camel Got His Hump: Word Search

T	H	T	O	S	E	F	S
T	R	O	T	H	H	E	N
C	S	N	R	O	H	T	N
E	A	S	E	R	H	C	I
T	O	M	S	S	O	H	J
D	S	E	E	E	G	O	D
O	R	G	D	L	T	M	D
H	U	M	P	E	T	U	E

Words to find:

camel	hump	desert
thorns	horse	dog
Djinn	trot	fetch

Jack and the Beanstalk

(The following can also be done orally, with the children raising their hands to respond.)

Find Someone Who!

Discover what your group has in common with the characters and places in *Jack and the Beanstalk*. Find a different name from the class or group for each item. The winner is the first to complete all eight items. The winner will then read each item and the person whose name is on each line will stand to verify that he or she can actually qualify for the item.

Find someone who . . .

1. Has seen a real cow.   _____

2. Has a first or last name that starts with J.   _____

3. Knows what bartering means.   _____

4. Can name two musical instruments.   _____

5. Can name two things louder than a giant's
   roar.   _____

6. Can name three garden vegetables.   _____

7. Likes eggs for breakfast.   _____

8. Can name two words that rhyme with
   BEAN.   _____

Storyteller's Introduction to *Jack and the Beanstalk*

The children call out "OH, NO!" when the storyteller raises his or her left hand and "OH, YES!" when the storyteller raises his or her right hand.

Storyteller: There once was a lad named Jack who was not very bright. He traded his mother's cow for five beans. Would you do that?

Children: OH, NO!

Storyteller: His mother was so angry she threw the beans away, and the next morning mother and Jack found a beanstalk so tall that it reached into the clouds. Should Jack climb the beanstalk?

Children: OH, YES!

Storyteller: Up the beanstalk Jack went, where he found a castle and was met at the door by the giant's wife. Jack was hungry, so being a kind woman she gave him some bread and cheese. Then she heard the giant coming.

> Fee fi fo fum
> I smell the blood of an Englishman
> Be he alive or be he dead
> I'll grind his bones to make my bread.

Should the giant's wife let the giant find Jack?

Children: OH, NO!

Storyteller: The giant's' wife hid Jack in the oven. After the giant had eaten, he counted his bags of gold and asked his wife to bring him his hen that laid golden eggs, and his golden harp that played such sweet music that the giant went to sleep. Should Jack take the giant's gold?

Children: OH, YES!

Storyteller: Jack not only took the gold in two more trips, but he took the hen and harp as well. On the third trip the giant awoke and chased Jack, who scrambled down the beanstalk with the giant close behind. Should the giant catch Jack?

Children: OH, NO!

Storyteller: You are right. Mother brought an axe and they chopped down the beanstalk so the giant could not follow Jack. With the bag of gold and the hen that laid a golden egg each day, Jack and his mother were no longer poor and they lived happily ever after.

Jack and the Beanstalk: The Films

Duvall, Shelley, prod. 1982. *Jack and the Beanstalk.* Faerie Tale Theatre. Starring Dennis Christopher, Katherine Helmond, Elliott Gould, Jean Stapleton. Live action full-color film. 60 minutes. All ages. Faithful to the original tale. Distributed by Fox Video.

Hanna-Barbera, prod. 1961. *Jack and the Beanstalk.* Animated color film with live action. 51 minutes. Ages 6–10. A musical version with Gene Kelley that varies from the original tale, when a merchant sells the beans to Jack and goes to the giant's castle with him. Released on laser disc 1966. Distributed by Hanna-Barbera Home Video.

Katsumi Furukaw/Henstooth Video, prod. 2005. *Jack and the Beanstalk.* Voices of Jack Grimes, Corinne Orr, Billie Lou Watt. Animated color film. 93 minutes. Ages 6–10. Subtitled in Japanese/English. Available from Amazon.com and Barnes&Noble.com.

Rabbit Ears Productions, prod. 1991. *Jack and the Beanstalk.* Narrated by Michael Palin. Animated color film. 28 minutes. Ages 4–8. Faithful to the original tale except for the ending, when Jack marries a princess. Distributed by Universal Distribution Corporation.

Screen Media, prod. 2010. *Jack and the Beanstalk.* Starring Gilbert Gottfried, Chevy Chase, Christopher Lloyd. Live action color film. 94 minutes. Ages 6–10. Available from Amazon.com and Barnes&Noble.com.

Free viewing of musical version available on the Internet via YouTube: *Jack and the Beanstalk*, http://www.youtube.com/watch?v=pf9cVnfyhjM, running time 4:14.

Jack and the Beanstalk: The Books

Benaduce, Ann. 1999. *Jack and the Beanstalk.* Illustrated by Gennady Spirin. New York: Philomel.

Cech, John. 2008. *Jack and the Beanstalk.* Illustrated by Robert Mackenzie. New York: Sterling.

Galdone, Paul. 1982. *Jack and the Beanstalk.* New York: Sandpiper.

Howe, John, illus. 1988. *Jack and the Beanstalk.* New York: Little, Brown and Company.

Jacobs, Joseph. 1977. *Jack and the Beanstalk.* Illustrated by Jan Pienkowski. Boston: Crowell.

Kellogg, Steven. 1991. *Jack and the Beanstalk.* New York: William Morrow.

Mayer, Mercer. 2010. *Jack and the Beanstalk: A Lift-the-Flap Book.* Little Critter Series. New York: Sterling.

Moore, Maggie. 2003. *Jack and the Beanstalk.* Illustrated by Steve Cox. Mankato, MN: Picture Window Books.

Nathan, Stella Williams, illus. 1990. *Jack and the Beanstalk.* Racine, WI: Western Publishing.

Nesbit, Edith. 2006. *Jack and the Beanstalk.* Illustrated by Matt Tavares. N.p.: Coward.

O'Ryan, Ellie. 2009. *Jack and the Beanstalk.* New York: Grosset and Dunlap.

Ottolenghi, Carol. 2002. *Jack and the Beanstalk.* Worthington, OH: Brighter Child.

Vagnozzi, Barbara. 2007. *Jack and the Beanstalk.* Flip-Up Fairy Tales. Swindon Wiltshire, UK: Child's Play.

Jack and the Beanstalk: I HAVE, WHO HAS Game

Directions: Cut all the cards apart. Each player gets one card. Begin with the question preceded by an asterisk (*). The student with the answer card responds.

I HAVE: Jack's mother brought an axe and Jack chopped down the beanstalk. *WHO HAS: Why did Jack's mother want to sell the cow?	I HAVE: The giant counted the coins in his money bags. WHO HAS: What did Jack do when the giant fell asleep?
I HAVE: They were poor and the cow had stopped giving milk. WHO HAS: What did Jack get for the cow and what did his mother do?	I HAVE: Jack took a money bag and climbed down the beanstalk. WHO HAS: What did Jack steal on his second trip to the giant's castle?
I HAVE: Jack got magic beans for the cow and his mother threw them away. WHO HAS: What did Jack and his mother find the next morning?	I HAVE: On trip two, Jack stole the giant's hen that laid golden eggs. WHO HAS: What did Jack steal on the third trip to the giant's castle?
I HAVE: They found a beanstalk that grew up into the clouds. WHO HAS: What did Jack find when he climbed the beanstalk?	I HAVE: On the third trip Jack stole the giant's golden harp. WHO HAS: What happened when the giant awoke and saw Jack stealing his harp?
I HAVE: He found the giant's castle, then was given food and hidden in the oven by the giant's wife. WHO HAS: What did the giant do after his meal?	I HAVE: The giant chased Jack. WHO HAS: Why didn't the giant catch Jack?

Jack and the Beanstalk: Library Treasure Hunt

Go to the children's nonfiction shelves. Look for each number on the spine of the books. What is each book about? That is the missing word. Write it on the line after the number. The player who finds all of the missing words first is the winner.

1. Jack received five beans for a 637. _____	2. The man told Jack the beans were 793.8. _____
3. After dinner the giant counted his 332.4. _____	4. The giant had a magic 636.5. _____
5. The harp made beautiful 784.19. _____	6. Jack and the Beanstalk is the type of story called a 398. _____

Key: 1. cow; 2. magic; 3. money; 4. hen; 5. music; 6. fairy tale

Jack and the Beanstalk: Word Search

T	N	O	J	P	H	H	G	A
B	K	D	L	O	G	E	L	J
H	I	O	H	H	I	R	N	E
B	E	T	M	E	A	L	K	L
G	E	G	J	O	N	R	C	D
A	T	A	A	J	T	O	P	S
H	C	G	N	I	W	H	D	S
K	L	A	T	S	N	A	E	B
A	A	H	C	A	A	O	S	R

Words to find:

Jack	mother	beans
cow	hen	harp
gold	giant	beanstalk

The Little Red Hen

(The following can also be done orally, with the children raising their hands to respond.)

Find Someone Who!

Discover what your group has in common with the characters and places in *The Little Red Hen*. Find a different name from the class or group for each item. The winner is the first to complete all eight items. The winner will then read each item and the person whose name is on each line will stand to verify that he or she can actually qualify for the item.

Find someone who . . .

1. Has planted a seed. _____

2. Has weeded a garden. _____

3. Has helped someone bake bread. _____

4. Has a cat for a pet. _____

5. Has fed a pig. _____

6. Can make a noise like a goose. _____

7. Has washed dishes. _____

8. Has had a hen for a pet. _____

Storyteller's Introduction to *The Little Red Hen*

Children practice these lines, which they will say at a signal from the storyteller:

But they all told her NO!
And that was that!

Storyteller:
"It takes wheat
To make bread,"
The Little Red Hen said.
"Come help
Plant the seeds
And pull up
The weeds,"
She said
To the goose
And the pig
And the cat.

Audience:
But they all told her NO!
And that was that!

Storyteller:
"Who will help
Cut the wheat
To take to
The mill
To grind
Into flour?
Tell me
Who will?"
She said
To the goose
And the pig
And the cat.

Audience:
But they all told her NO!
And that was that!

Storyteller:
"I'll take home
The flour
This very hour.
Who will help
Bake the bread?"
The Little Red Hen said
To the goose
And the pig
And the cat.

Audience:
But they all told her NO!
And that was that!

Storyteller:
The Little
Red Hen
Planted
The seeds,
Tended
The garden,
Pulled up
The weeds,
Carted
The wheat

Off to
The mill,
Took flour
Home,
Baked bread
Until
Warm golden
Slices
Were ready
To eat.
Then the others
Showed up
To partake
Of the treat.
But the Little
Red Hen told
The goose,
Pig and cat,
"I'll eat it myself!"
And that was that.

The Little Red Hen: The Films

Baby Bumblebee Studios, prod. 2005. *Kids Flix, Volume 1.* Animated color film. 52 minutes. Ages 4–6. Features "Humpty Dumpty," "The Little Red Hen," and "The Three Little Pigs." Available from Amazon.com.

Coronet, prod. 1950. *The Little Red Hen.* Live action color film mixed with drawings. 10 minutes. Ages 3–6. Distributed by Coronet/MTI Film and Video.

Family Home Entertainment, prod. 1995. *Papa Beaver's Story Time 2: Little Red Hen.* Animated color film. 47 minutes. Ages 4–8. Available from Amazon.com.

Free viewing on the Internet via YouTube: *Little Red Hen,* http://www.youtube .com/watch?v=YppnQkP2PXE, running time 9:35; http://www.youtube.com/ watch?v=cJDwq_VLkKQ, running time 7:03; and http://www.youtube.com/ watch?v=zr-yQGD9eAA, running time 7:16.

The Little Red Hen: The Books

Barton, Byron, illus. 1993. *The Little Red Hen.* New York: HarperCollins.

Forest, Heather. 2006. *The Little Red Hen.* Illustrated by Susan Gaber. Atlanta, GA: August House LittleFolk.

Galdone, Paul, illus. 1993. *The Little Red Hen.* New York: Clarion Books.

Garneer, Alan. 1997. *The Little Red Hen.* New York: DK.

Jones, Christianne C. 2005. *The Little Red Hen.* Illustrated by Natalie Magnuson. Mankato, MN: Picture Window Books.

Kimmelman, Leslie. 2010. *The Little Red Hen and the Passover Matzah.* Illustrated by Paul Meisel. New York: Holiday House.

Pinkney, Jerry, illus. 1996. *The Little Red Hen.* New York: Dial.

Spengler, Kenneth. 2007. *Little Red Hen Gets Help.* Illustrated by Margaret Spengler. New York: Harcourt.

Sturges, Philemon. 2009. *The Little Red Hen Makes a Pizza.* Illustrated by Amy Walrod. New York: Dutton Children's Books.

Ziefert, Harriet. 1995. *The Little Red Hen.* New York: Viking.

The Little Red Hen: I HAVE, WHO HAS Game

Directions: Cut all the cards apart. Each player gets one card. Begin with the question preceded by an asterisk (*). The student with the answer card responds.

I HAVE: The Little Red Hen ate the bread all by herself. *WHO HAS: What did the Little Red Hen find on her walk?	I HAVE: The pig, cat, and goose refused to help harvest the wheat. WHO HAS: What did the pig, cat, and goose say when the Little Red Hen asked for help in taking the grain to the mill?
I HAVE: The Little Red Hen found grains of wheat. WHO HAS: What did the Little Red Hen want to do with the grains of wheat?	I HAVE: The pig, cat, and goose refused to help take the grain to the mill. WHO HAS: What did the pig, cat, and goose say when the Little Red Hen asked for help in baking the bread?
I HAVE: The Little Red Hen wanted to plant the grains of wheat. WHO HAS: Who did the Little Red Hen ask to help her plant the grains of wheat?	I HAVE: The pig, cat, and goose refused to help bake the bread. WHO HAS: What happened when the bread was baked and ready to eat?
I HAVE: The Little Red Hen asked the cat, the pig, and the goose for help. WHO HAS: What did the cat, pig, and goose tell the Little Red Hen?	I HAVE: The pig, cat, and goose all were ready to eat the freshly baked bread. WHO HAS: What did the Little Red Hen do?
I HAVE: They told the Little Red Hen they would not help plant the wheat. WHO HAS: What did the pig, cat, and goose say when the Little Red Hen asked for help in harvesting the wheat?	I HAVE: The Little Red Hen did not share the freshly baked bread. WHO HAS: Who ate the freshly baked bread?

The Little Red Hen: Library Treasure Hunt

Go to the children's nonfiction shelves. Look for each number on the spine of the books. What is each book about? That is the missing word. Write it on the line after the number. The player who finds all of the missing words first is the winner.

1. The Little Red Hen planted 581.4 in her garden. _____	2. The mill would grind the 633.1 into flour. _____
3. The 636.8 did not help the Little Red Hen. _____	4. The 636.4 did not help the Little Red Hen. _____
5. The main character in this story is a 636.5. _____	6. The Little Red Hen ate the 641.8 all by herself. _____

Key: 1. seeds; 2. wheat; 3. cat; 4. pig; 5. hen; 6. bread

The Little Red Hen: Word Search

P	A	U	F	S	T	A
I	W	R	D	N	E	N
G	H	E	U	D	E	L
C	E	S	O	O	G	H
W	A	M	I	L	L	B
F	T	A	C	E	E	F
B	R	E	A	D	T	P

Words to find:

hen	goose	cat
wheat	weeds	pig
flour	bread	mill

Little Red Riding Hood

(The following can also be done orally, with the children raising their hands to respond.)

Find Someone Who!

Discover what your group has in common with the characters and places in *Little Red Riding Hood*. Find a different name from the class or group for each item. The winner is the first to complete all eight items. The winner will then read each item and the person whose name is on each line will stand to verify that he or she can actually qualify for the item.

Find someone who...

1. Has taken a gift to his or her grandmother.   _____

2. Has walked alone in the woods.   _____

3. Has seen a real wolf.   _____

4. Has helped someone bake bread.   _____

5. Is wearing something red.   _____

6. Has a name that starts with R.   _____

7. Can name two words that rhyme with
   HOOD.   _____

8. Has two grandmothers.   _____

Storyteller's Introduction to *Little Red Riding Hood*

At a signal from the storyteller, **the audience will respond by repeating the bold lines**.

Now Granny was hungry
But never would ask it
Of Red Riding Hood
To bring her a basket
Filled to the top
With good things to eat
Like apples and oranges
And fresh bread and meat.

But the child was sweet,
Yes, the child was good,
So she set out to take
Her Granny some food.
She skipped through the woods
On a bright sunny day
Till a mean wolf appeared
In the path on her way.

"Where are you going?"
He spoke loud and clear.
"I'm taking these goodies
to Grandmother dear."
The wolf spoke again,
"At this early hour
Why don't you take Granny
A freshly picked flower?"

"Oh, a flower," she said,
"I'll take Granny one.
Look how pretty they bloom
In the morning sun."
So the wolf left the girl
And ran through the wood
To gobble up Granny
As fast as he could.

But the child was not fooled
The child was quite wise
She saw that the wolf
Had donned a disguise
The wolf tried to eat her,
He grabbed her but missed
She swung her arm back
And let go with her fist.

He choked and he sneezed
His wolf lungs to clear
Then with one mighty cough
Up came Grandmother dear
So the next time you take
Your Granny a treat
Don't stop on the path
For a wolf you might meet.

Little Red Riding Hood: The Films

DEFA Studios, prod. 1979. *Little Red Riding Hood.* Animated color film. 13 minutes. Ages 5–8. Faithful re-creation of the original tale. Distributed by Coronet/MTI Film and Video.

Duvall, Shelley, prod. 1983. *Little Red Riding Hood.* Faerie Tale Theatre. Starring Mary Steenbergen, Malcolm McDowell, Diane Ladd. Live action color film. 60 minutes. Ages 5–12. Faithful re-creation of the original tale. Distributed by Fox Video.

Golan-Globus Productions, prod. 1989. *Little Red Riding Hood.* Live action color film. 84 minutes. Ages 6–12. Musical adaptation with considerable departure from the original tale. Distributed by Canon Video.

Harryhausen, Ray, prod. 1958. *Little Red Riding Hood.* Puppet-animated color film. 9 minutes. Ages 5–8. Faithful re-creation of the original tale. Distributed by Phoenix/BFA Films and Video.

New World Video, prod. 1979. *The Brothers Grimm Fairy Tales.* Animated color film. 35 minutes. Ages 5–8. Also includes "The Seven Ravens." Available from Amazon.com.

Free viewing on the Internet via YouTube: *Little Red Riding Hood,* http://www.youtube .com/watch?v=9NRyB04Mtvc, running time 4:58.

Little Red Riding Hood: The Books

Bolam, Emily, illus. 2000. *Little Red Riding Hood.* New York: Viking.

Daly, Niki. 2007. *Pretty Salma: A Little Red Riding Hood Story from Africa.* New York: Clarion.

Evetts-Secker, Josephine. 2004. *Little Red Riding Hood.* Illustrated by Nicoletta Ceccoli. Cambridge, MA: Barefoot Books.

Hayano, Michiyo. 2009. *Little Red Riding Hood.* Milwaukie, OR: Dark Horse Comics.

Hillert, Margaret. 2006. *Little Red Riding Hood.* Illustrated by Gwen Connelly. Chicago: Norwood House Press.

Hyman, Trina Schart. 1988. *Little Red Riding Hood.* New York: Holiday House.

Lavreys, Debbie. 2008. *Little Red Riding Hood.* New York: Clavis.

Martin, Jean-Francois, illus. 1998. *Little Red Riding Hood: A Fairy Tale by Grimm.* New York: Abbeville Kids.

McBratney, Sam. 2004. *Little Red Riding Hood.* Illustrated by Emma Chichester Clark. London: Hodder Children's.

Moore, Maggie. 2003. *Little Red Riding Hood.* Illustrated by Paula Knight. Mankato, MN: Picture Window Books.

Pinkney, Jerry. 2007. *Little Red Riding Hood.* New York: Little, Brown and Company.

Polette, Keith. 2004. *Isabelle and the Hungry Coyote.* Illustrated by Esther Szegedy. McHenry, IL: Raven Tree Press.

Spirin, Gennady. 2010. *Little Red Riding Hood.* Tarrytown, NY: Marshall Cavendish.

Watts, Bernadette. 2009. *Little Red Riding Hood.* New York: North-South.

Wisnewski, Andrea. 2006. *Little Red Riding Hood.* Boston: David R. Godine.

Little Red Riding Hood: I HAVE, WHO HAS Game

Directions: Cut all the cards apart. Each player gets one card. Begin with the question preceded by an asterisk (*). The student with the answer card responds.

I HAVE: She gave Grandmother the basket of goodies. *WHO HAS: How did Red Riding Hood get her name?	I HAVE: Red Riding Hood told the wolf she was going to her grandmother's. WHO HAS: How did the wolf get to the grandmother's house first?
I HAVE: Her mother made her a red riding hood. WHO HAS: What did Red Riding Hood's mother ask her to do?	I HAVE: Red Riding Hood stopped to pick flowers on the way. WHO HAS: What happened to Grandmother when she saw the wolf?
I HAVE: Mother asked Red Riding Hood to take a basket of goodies to her ill grandmother. WHO HAS: What did Red Riding Hood have to go through to get to her grandmother's?	I HAVE: The wolf gobbled up Grandmother. WHO HAS: What happened when Red Riding Hood arrived at her grandmother's house?
I HAVE: Red Riding Hood had to go through the woods to get to her grandmother's. WHO HAS: Who did Red Riding Hood meet in the woods?	I HAVE: The wolf pretended to be Grandmother. WHO HAS: What happened when the wolf tried to eat Red Riding Hood?
I HAVE: Red Riding Hood met a wolf in the woods. WHO HAS: What did Red Riding Hood say when the wolf asked her where she was going?	I HAVE: She hit the wolf, who then coughed up Grandmother. WHO HAS: What did Red Riding Hood do then?

Little Red Riding Hood: Library Treasure Hunt

Go to the children's nonfiction shelves. Look for each number on the spine of the books. What is each book about? That is the missing word. Write it on the line after the number. The player who finds all of the missing words first is the winner.

1. Red Riding Hood was taking 613.2 to her Grandmother. _____	2. Red Riding Hood had to go through the 577.3 to get to Grandmother's house. _____
3. Red Riding Hood had some 641.8 in her basket. _____	4. Red Riding Hood met a 599.77 in the woods. _____
5. Red Riding Hood stopped to pick some 582.13. _____	6. This story is known as a 398.2. _____

Key: 1. food; 2. forest; 3. bread; 4. wolf; 5. flowers; 6. fairy tale

Little Red Riding Hood: Word Search

A	R	E	D	Y	R	G	N
T	E	K	S	A	B	D	O
E	H	H	E	M	S	R	D
E	T	A	U	D	S	O	N
T	O	G	O	N	E	E	U
H	M	O	I	A	T	Y	T
S	W	A	S	R	E	E	G
W	O	L	F	G	L	S	R

Words to find:

basket	mother	girl
woods	wolf	grandma
hunter	eyes	teeth

Peter and the Wolf

(By Sergei Prokofiev)

(The following can also be done orally, with the children raising their hands to respond.)

Find Someone Who!

Discover what your group has in common with the characters and places in *Peter and the Wolf.* Find a different name from the class or group for each item. The winner is the first to complete all eight items. The winner will then read each item and the person whose name is on each line will stand to verify that he or she can actually qualify for the item.

Find someone who . . .

1. Has two grandfathers. _____

2. Likes to take long walks. _____

3. Has climbed a tree. _____

4. Has visited a zoo. _____

5. Has seen a real wolf. _____

6. Can make a noise like a duck. _____

7. Can name two musical instruments. _____

8. Has a first name that begins with P. _____

Storyteller's Introduction to *Peter and the Wolf*

Divide the group into four parts: birds, ducks, wolves, cats. At a signal from the storyteller, birds will say, "Chirp, chirp, chirp, chirp!," ducks will say, "Quack, quack, quack, quack!," cats will say, "Meow! Meow!," and wolves will say, "Grrr, Grrr, Grrr, Grrr."

Storyteller: Young Peter had been warned by his grandfather not to go into the meadow for there might be wolves there. Peter went to the meadow anyway and the first thing he heard was a bird arguing with a duck.

Birds: Chirp, chirp, chirp, chirp!
Ducks: Quack, quack, quack, quack!

Storyteller: The bird was so busy arguing with the duck that she did not see the cat sneaking up behind her.

Cats: Meow! Meow!

Storyteller: Peter shouted, "Look out!" and the bird flew up in the tree. The cat climbed the tree and the duck waddled out of the pond.

(All together)
Birds: Chirp, chirp, chirp, chirp!
Ducks: Quack, quack, quack, quack!
Cats: Meow! Meow!

Storyteller: Just then a wolf came out of the woods, grabbed the duck, and swallowed her.

(All together)
Wolves: Grrrr, Grrr, Grrr, Grrr.
Ducks: Quack, quack, quack, quack!

Storyteller: Peter saw what was happening. He ran into the house. He got a long rope. He climbed a stone wall to reach one of the branches of the tree. The bird was on one branch.

Birds: Chirp, chirp, chirp, chirp!

Storyteller: The cat was on another branch.

Cats: Meow! Meow!

Storyteller: And Peter with the rope was on a third branch. What do you suppose Peter plans to do? Let's watch the film *(or read the story)* and find out.

Peter and the Wolf: The Films

Columbia Tri Star, prod. 1996. *Peter and the Wolf.* Starring Kirstie Alley, Lloyd Bridges. Color film with live action and animation. 49 minutes. Ages 5–adult. Faithful to the original in text and orchestration. Available from Amazon.com and Barnes&Noble.com.

Dewhurst, Alan, and Hugh Welchman, prods. 2006. *Peter and the Wolf.* Color film with puppet animation. 32 minutes. Ages 5–adult. Faithful to the original in text and orchestration. Distributed by Breakthru Films.

Walt Disney Studios, prod. 1946. *Peter and the Wolf.* Narrated by Sterling Holloway. Animated color film. 30 minutes. Ages 5–adult. Faithful to the original in text and orchestration. Available from Amazon.com and Barnes&Noble.com.

Free viewing on the Internet via YouTube: *Peter and the Wolf,* http://www.youtube.com/watch?v=ILI3s7Wonvg, running time 7:36 and 7:22, ages 4–8.

Peter and the Wolf: The Books

Beck, Ian. 1995. *Peter and the Wolf.* London: Transworld Publishers.

Daugherty, George, and Janis Diamond. 1994. *Chuck Jones' Peter and the Wolf.* New York: Warner.

Hastings, Selina. 2002. *Peter and the Wolf.* Illustrated by Reg Cartwright. New York: Walker.

Herndon, Lynne Doherty. 2003. *Peter and the Wolf.* Illustrated by Rhian James and Kathy Jakeman. Upper Saddle River, NJ: Pearson ESL.

Prado, Miguelanxo. 1998. *Peter and the Wolf.* New York: NBM.

Prokofiev, Sergei. 1972. *Peter and the Wolf.* New York: Disney Book Club/Random House.

Prokofiev, Sergei. 1982. *Peter and the Wolf.* Illustrated by Charles Mikolaycak. New York: Viking.

Prokofiev, Sergei. 2000. *Peter and the Wolf.* Illustrated by Vladimir Vagin. New York: Scholastic.

Prokofiev, Sergei. 2008. *Peter and the Wolf.* Illustrated by Chris Raschka. New York: Atheneum Books for Young Readers.

Schulman, Janet. 2004. *Peter and the Wolf.* Illustrated by Peter Malone. New York: Knopf.

Peter and the Wolf: I HAVE, WHO HAS Game

Directions: Cut all the cards apart. Each player gets one card. Begin with the question preceded by an asterisk (*). The student with the answer card responds.

I HAVE: Peter said, "Don't shoot." They took the wolf to the zoo. *WHO HAS: Where was Peter warned not to go?	I HAVE: Grandfather was angry because Peter disobeyed him. WHO HAS: What did Grandfather do?
I HAVE: Peter was warned by his grandfather not to go to the meadow. WHO HAS: What did Peter see first in the meadow.	I HAVE: Grandfather took Peter in the house and locked the gate. WHO HAS: What did Peter see from his window?
I HAVE: Peter saw a duck in a pond arguing with a bird that hopped along the edge of the pond. WHO HAS: Why did Peter shout, "Look out!"	I HAVE: Peter saw a wolf catch the duck. He saw a bird and cat up in a tree. WHO HAS: What did Peter do?
I HAVE: Peter saw a cat sneaking up on the bird to catch it. WHO HAS: What did the bird do when the cat was near?	I HAVE: Peter got a rope, climbed the tree, and, with the help of the bird, caught the wolf by the tail. WHO HAS: Who came out of the woods to help Peter?
I HAVE: The bird flew up in a tree. WHO HAS: Who came out of the house and why was he angry?	I HAVE: Two hunters with guns came out to help Peter. WHO HAS: What did Peter say, and what happened to the wolf?

Peter and the Wolf: Library Treasure Hunt

Go to the children's nonfiction shelves. Look for each number on the spine of the books. What is each book about? That is the missing word. Write it on the line after the number. The player who finds all of the missing words first is the winner.

1. Sergei Prokofiev is a composer from the country of 947.086. _____	2. Peter saw two 598 in the meadow. _____
3. Peter yelled to the bird, "Look out!" when he saw a 636.8. _____	4. At the edge of the meadow was a 577.3. _____
5. Peter was determined to catch the 599.77. _____	6. They took the wolf to the 590.73. _____

Key: 1. Russia; 2. birds; 3. cat; 4. forest; 5. wolf; 6. zoo

Peter and the Wolf: Word Search

W	R	O	F	R	W	D
R	O	P	E	L	T	O
C	T	E	E	R	O	W
C	A	T	E	Z	D	W
S	R	E	T	N	U	H
T	D	R	I	B	C	E
O	E	R	Z	D	K	P

Words to find:

Peter	bird	duck
cat	wolf	tree
rope	zoo	hunters

The Pied Piper of Hamelin

(By Robert Browning)

(The following can also be done orally, with the children raising their hands to respond.)

Find Someone Who!

Discover what your group has in common with the characters and places in *The Pied Piper of Hamelin.* Find a different name from the class or group for each item. The winner is the first to complete all eight items. The winner will then read each item and the person whose name is on each line will stand to verify that he or she can actually qualify for the item.

Find someone who . . .

1. Lives or has lived in a small town. _____

2. Can find Germany on a map. _____

3. Can play an instrument. _____

4. Has kept a promise. _____

5. Can name five words that rhyme with
   RAT. _____

6. Has climbed a mountain. _____

7. Can name four words that begin with the
   letter P. _____

8. Can name something made of gold. _____

Storyteller's Introduction to *The Pied Piper of Hamelin*

Audience chants this refrain at a signal from the storyteller:

Rats in the pantry
Rats on the stair
Fat rats, skinny rats, everywhere!

Storyteller:
From early morn
Till the sun went down
Rats took over
Hamelin town.

Audience:
Rats in the pantry
Rats on the stair
Fat rats, skinny rats, everywhere!

Storyteller:
Hurry, hurry,
Find some cats.
We must get rid
Of these awful rats.
But sad to say
There were no cats,
Just lots and lots
Of pesky rats.

Audience:
Rats in the pantry
Rats on the stair
Fat rats, skinny rats, everywhere!

Storyteller:
Then into town
A Piper strolled
To rid the rats
If paid in gold.

Audience:
Rats in the pantry
Rats on the stair
Fat rats, skinny rats, everywhere!

Storyteller:
The Mayor said, Yes,
They'd pay the fee,
Once the town
Of rats was free.
Rats then followed
His tune so gay
And into the river
Were swept away.
The Piper said
In words so bold,
"Please, Sir, I'll
Now take my gold."
The Mayor refused
The Piper to pay,
So the Piper took
The children away.
Now in the streets
Both up and down
Rats are again
In Hamelin Town.

Audience:
Rats in the pantry
Rats on the stair
Fat rats, skinny rats, everywhere!

The Pied Piper of Hamelin: The Films

Argo Sight and Sound, prod. 1970. *The Pied Piper of Hamelin.* Narrated by Peter Ustinov. Animated color film. 17 minutes. Ages 8–12. Faithful rendition of the original Browning tale. Distributed by Phoenix/BFA Films and Video.

Coronet, prod. 1980. *The Pied Piper of Hamelin.* Animated color film. 11 minutes. Ages 8–12. Faithful rendition of the original Browning tale. Distributed by Coronet/MTI Film and Video.

Duvall, Shelley, prod. 1982. *The Pied Piper of Hamelin.* Faerie Tale Theatre. Live action color film. 60 minutes. Ages 8–adult. Introductory material precedes faithful rendition of the original Browning tale. Distributed by Fox Video.

Pied Piper Productions, prod. 1983. *The Pied Piper of Hamelin.* Narrated by Orson Wells. Color film with limited animation. 18 minutes. Ages 8–12. Faithful rendition of the original Browning tale. Available from Amazon.com.

Walt Disney, prod. 1986. *The Pied Piper.* Animated color film. 8 minutes. Ages 4–8. Ending of the original tale changed. Distributed by Coronet/MTI Film and Video.

Free viewing on the Internet via Youtube: *The Pied Piper of Hamelin,* http://www.youtube.com/watch?v=bkYRGlKzAvY, running time 10:43, ages 4–8.

The Pied Piper of Hamelin: The Books

Barkow, Henriette. 2002. *The Pied Piper.* Illustrated by Roland Dry. London: Mantra.

Blair, Eric. 2005. *The Pied Piper of Hamelin.* Illustrated by Ben Peterson. Mankato, MN: Picture Window Books.

Browning, Robert. 1993. *The Pied Piper of Hamelin.* Illustrated by Kate Greenaway. New York: Random House.

Browning, Robert. 1993. *The Pied Piper of Hamelin.* Illustrated by Michele Lemieux. New York: Morrow.

Browning, Robert. 2008. *The Pied Piper of Hamelin.* Illustrated by Hope Dunlap. Chapel Hill, NC: Yesterday's Classics.

Corrin, Sara, and Stephen Corrin. 1991. *The Pied Piper of Hamelin.* Illustrated by Errol Le Cain. New York: Harcourt.

Impey, Rose. 1985. *The Pied Piper of Hamelin.* New York: Penguin.

Kellogg, Steven. 2009. *The Pied Piper's Magic.* New York: Dial Books for Young Readers.

Peen, Bud. 1999. *The Pied Piper of Hamelin.* New York: Abrams.

Schindler, Steven D. 1989. *The Pied Piper of Hamelin.* New York: Random House.

Tompert, Ann. 2002. *The Pied Piper of Peru.* Illustrated by Kestutis Kasparavicius. Honesdale, PA: Boyds Mills Press.

The Pied Piper of Hamelin: I HAVE, WHO HAS Game

Directions: Cut all the cards apart. Each player gets one card. Begin with the question preceded by an asterisk (*). The student with the answer card responds.

I HAVE: The mountain pass disappeared. *WHO HAS: What problem did the town of Hamelin have?	I HAVE: The Piper played his pipes and led the rats to the river. WHO HAS: What happened when the Piper asked for payment?
I HAVE: The town was overrun by rats. WHO HAS: What strange fellow strolled into town?	I HAVE: The Mayor and the Town Council refused to pay. WHO HAS: What did the Piper do when payment was refused?
I HAVE: The Pied Piper strolled into town. WHO HAS: What offer did the Piper make to the Town Council?	I HAVE: The Piper went through the streets piping his tune again. WHO HAS: Who followed the Piper this time?
I HAVE: The Piper offered to rid the town of rats for fifty pieces of gold. WHO HAS: What did Town Council do about his offer?	I HAVE: The children of Hamelin followed the Piper. WHO HAS: Where did the Piper lead the children?
I HAVE: The Council accepted the Piper's offer. WHO HAS: How did the Piper get rid of the rats?	I HAVE: The Piper led the children through a mountain pass. WHO HAS: Why couldn't the parents follow the children?

The Pied Piper of Hamelin: Library Treasure Hunt

Go to the children's nonfiction shelves. Look for each number on the spine of the books. What is each book about? That is the missing word. Write it on the line after the number. The player who finds all of the missing words first is the winner.

1. Hamelin Town was overrun with 599.35. _____	2. The Piper led the rats to the 577.6. _____
3. Robert Browning, the author of *The Pied Piper*, lived in 942. _____	4. The Piper made 784.19 with his pipes. _____
5. The Council refused to give the Piper the 332.4 they had promised. _____	6. The Piper led the children through a pass in the 551.4. _____

Key: 1. rats; 2. river; 3. England; 4. music; 5. money; 6. mountain

The Pied Piper of Hamelin: Word Search

R	M	M	M	R	R	H	E	Y	E
E	S	R	M	O	D	G	N	I	K
R	N	R	Y	P	E	E	H	I	S
P	M	A	E	I	R	N	N	M	R
S	M	T	O	D	I	R	P	O	A
S	E	S	L	L	L	I	P	N	O
E	P	I	E	D	P	I	P	E	R
D	H	M	L	E	Y	A	U	Y	A
C	A	P	S	R	O	I	M	G	O
H	H	E	G	L	G	E	P	R	H

Words to find:

Pied Piper	Hamelin	children
rats	mayor	guilders
pipes	money	kingdom

Puss in Boots

(The following can also be done orally, with the children raising their hands to respond.)

Find Someone Who!

Discover what your group has in common with the characters and places in *Puss in Boots*. Find a different name from the class or group for each item. The winner is the first to complete all eight items. The winner will then read each item and the person whose name is on each line will stand to verify that he or she can actually qualify for the item.

Find someone who . . .

1. Likes to go swimming.   _____

2. Has a cat for a pet.   _____

3. Is the youngest child.   _____

4. Has a pair of boots.   _____

5. Has seen a real lion.   _____

6. Has caught a mouse.   _____

7. Has a first or last name that begins with P. _____

8. Can name another story with a princess.   _____

Storyteller's Introduction to *Puss in Boots*

At a signal from the storyteller, **the audience will repeat the last two lines of each verse.**

A miller left
To each son
A small gift
For each one.
One a donkey
Two a mill
Nothing left
For third son till
Fine young fellow
Very poor
Received a cat
Nothing more.

Cat hung a bag
Round his neck
Saw a bird
Hunt and peck
Caught the bird
Just the thing
Took the bird
To the king.
Brought more gifts
From his master
Fooled the king
With a disaster.

Cat told the boy,
"Pretend to drown
King will pass
By to town."
Carriage stops
Saves the lad
Given clothing
Richly clad.
Cat becomes
Loud broadcaster:
"ALL LAND BELONGS
TO MY MASTER!"

Cat runs ahead
To ogre's dwelling
Hears loud sound
Ogre yelling.
Ogre turns self
To a rat
Eaten quickly
By the cat.
King arrives
At house so fine.
Lad tells him,
"House is mine."

"Well," said King,
"Is it true
This castle does
Belong to you
As well as all
Surrounding land?
I'll give to you
My daughter's hand.
I trust her to
Your tender care."
The lad then wed
The princess fair
The lad indeed
A lucky one.
No more to tell
This tale is done.

Puss in Boots: The Films

Coronet, prod. 1980. *Puss in Boots.* Color film with limited animation. 11 minutes. Ages 5–10. A short but accurate version of the classic tale. Distributed by Coronet/MTI Film and Video.

Duvall, Shelley, prod. 1984. *Puss in Boots.* Faerie Tale Theatre. Starring Gregory Hines, Ben Vereen, Alfred Woodard. Live action color film. 60 minutes. Ages 6–12. Some slight changes from the traditional tale. Distributed by Fox Video.

Golan-Globus Productions, prod. 2005. *Puss in Boots.* Starring Christopher Walken, Jason Connery, Amon Meskin. Live action color film. 96 minutes. Ages 5–12. A musical version of the classic tale. Distributed by MGM Video. Available from Amazon.com and Barnes&Noble.com.

Good Times Video, prod. 2005. *Puss in Boots.* Animated color film. 50 minutes. Ages 5–10. Follows the traditional tale closely. Available from Amazon.com and Barnes&Noble.com.

Olaza Entertainment, prod. 1999. *Puss in Boots.* Voices of Michael York, Vivian Schilling, Dan Haggerty, Judge Reinhold. Animated color film. 65 minutes. Ages 5–10. Follows the story line with addition of songs. Available from Amazon.com and Barnes&Noble.com.

Free viewing of Parts 1–4 on the Internet via YouTube: *Puss in Boots,* http://www.youtube.com/watch?v=S3yIkcaS8yg, running time 22:38, ages 4–8.

Puss in Boots: The Books

Arthur, Malcolm, trans. 2007. *Puss in Boots.* Illustrated by Fred Marcellino. New York: Farrar, Straus, and Giroux.

Blair, Eric. 2005. *Puss in Boots.* Illustrated by Todd Ouren. Mankato, MN: Picture Window Books.

Cech, John. 2010. *Puss in Boots.* Illustrated by Bernhard Oberdieck. New York: Sterling.

Galdone, Paul. 1979. *Puss in Boots.* New York: Clarion Books.

Jackson, Kathryn. 2009. *Puss in Boots.* Racine, WI: Western Publishing.

Kirstein, Lincoln. 1994. *Puss in Boots.* Illustrated by Alain Vaes. New York: Little, Brown and Company.

Light, Steven. 2002. *Puss in Boots.* New York: Harry N. Abrams.

McBain, Ed. 1994. *Puss in Boots.* New York: Grand Central Publishing.

Metaxas, Eric. 1992. *Puss in Boots.* Illustrated by Pierre Le-Tan. South Norwalk, CT: Rabbit Ears.

Patchett, Fiona. 2009. *Puss in Boots.* Illustrated by Teri Gower. London: Usborne.

Pullman, Philip. 2001. *Puss in Boots.* New York: Knopf.

Stockham, Jessica. 2007. *Puss in Boots.* Flip-Up Fairy Tales. Swindon, Wiltshire, UK: Child's Play.

Puss in Boots: I HAVE, WHO HAS Game

Directions: Cut all the cards apart. Each player gets one card. Begin with the question preceded by an asterisk (*). The student with the answer card responds.

I HAVE: The lad and the princess married and lived happily ever after. *WHO HAS: What did the youngest son receive from his father?	I HAVE: The lad was rescued and invited to ride in the carriage. WHO HAS: Why did the cat run ahead of the carriage?
I HAVE: The youngest son was left only a cat by his father. WHO HAS: What did the cat ask for?	I HAVE: The cat told the field hands to say that all the land belonged to his master. WHO HAS: What did the ogre do to show his power?
I HAVE: The cat asked for a bag and some boots. WHO HAS: What did the cat do with the bag?	I HAVE: The ogre turned himself into a lion. WHO HAS: What did the cat challenge the ogre to do next?
I HAVE: He caught birds and took them to the king as a gift from his master. WHO HAS: What did the lad do to get the king's attention?	I HAVE: The cat challenged the ogre to turn himself into a mouse. WHO HAS: What did the cat do to the mouse?
I HAVE: The cat told the lad to bathe in the pool and pretend he was drowning. WHO HAS: What did the king do when he saw the lad in the pool?	I HAVE: The cat ate the mouse, then claimed the ogre's castle belonged to his master. WHO HAS: How did the story end?

Puss in Boots: Library Treasure Hunt

Go to the children's nonfiction shelves. Look for each number on the spine of the books. What is each book about? That is the missing word. Write it on the line after the number. The player who finds all of the missing words first is the winner.

1. Puss in Boots is a tale from 944. _____	2. The youngest brother is helped by a 636.8. _____
3. The cat told the reapers that the 633.1 belonged to his master. _____	4. The cat told the lad to bathe in the 577.6. _____
5. The ogre lived in a 728.8. _____	6. The ogre changed himself into a 599.35. _____

Key: 1. France; 2. cat; 3. wheat; 4. river; 5. castle; 6. mouse

Puss in Boots: Word Search

O	T	M	E	I	T	E	P	S	A
I	D	A	O	G	R	E	A	P	R
G	P	M	I	L	L	E	R	E	E
G	G	R	A	B	B	I	T	G	G
R	O	T	B	D	N	S	R	N	O
E	C	O	R	C	A	O	I	S	K
R	A	A	E	M	M	K	D	P	P
C	A	S	T	O	O	B	G	N	N
R	S	E	E	T	P	E	E	R	M
A	S	T	R	L	S	P	T	D	P

Words to find:

miller	cat	master
boots	rabbit	king
partridge	ogre	princess

Rapunzel

(The following can also be done orally, with the children raising their hands to respond.)

Find Someone Who!

Discover what your group has in common with the characters and places in *Rapunzel*. Find a different name from the class or group for each item. The winner is the first to complete all eight items. The winner will then read each item and the person whose name is on each line will stand to verify that he or she can actually qualify for the item.

Find someone who . . .

1. Has hair longer than six inches. _____

2. Has a first name beginning with R. _____

3. Can name three garden vegetables. _____

4. Can name another tale with a witch. _____

5. Has recently had a haircut. _____

6. Can name three words that rhyme with HAIR. _____

7. Has kept a promise. _____

8. Has told someone a secret. _____

Storyteller's Introduction to *Rapunzel*

At a signal from the storyteller, thumbs up or thumbs down, audience members alternate responding with "That's good!" and "That's bad!"

Storyteller: A woman expecting a child longed for a taste of the rich green lettuce that grew in the garden beyond a tall fence. Her husband told her he would climb the fence and bring her some.

Audience: That's good!

Storyteller: No, that was bad because he was caught by a witch who owned the garden and who, if she wished, could take his life.

Audience: That's bad!

Storyteller: It was actually good because she did not harm him. Instead she gave him the lettuce for his wife and so he escaped unharmed.

Audience: That's good!

Storyteller: This was actually bad, for he had to promise her their first-born child, and when the child was born the witch came and took her away and shut her up in a tower with no steps or door and only a small window above.

Audience: That's bad!

Storyteller: Not really, because after a few years passed, a handsome prince who would never have met her otherwise rode near the tower and heard the girl singing. He saw the witch climb up her hair, and when the witch left he did the same.

Audience: That's good!

Storyteller: It was good for a short time but turned out to be bad, for when the witch heard about the prince she took Rapunzel away and hid her deep in the desert. The poor prince was blinded by thorns when he fell from the tower.

Audience: That's bad!

Storyteller: Yes, it was very bad. The poor blind prince wandered for years in misery, and the poor girl lived a lonely life in the desert. Will this fairy tale have a happy ending? Let's watch the film *(or read the story)* to find out.

Rapunzel: The Films

Duvall, Shelley, prod. 1982. *Rapunzel.* Faerie Tale Theatre. Starring Jeff Bridges, Shelley Duvall, Gena Rowlands, Roddy McDowell. Live action color film. 60 minutes. Ages 8–adult. Stays close to the original tale with very slight changes. Released on DVD 2004. Distributed by Fox Video.

Hanna-Barbera and Hallmark, prods. 1996. *Rapunzel.* Narrated by Olivia Newton-John. Animated color film. 30 minutes. Ages 4–8. Some smaller details in the story changed. Distributed by Hanna-Barbera Home Video.

Scholastic, prod. 2009. *Rapunzel and More Classic Fairy Tales.* Narrated by T. K. Animated color film. 87 minutes (total running time for all tales). Ages 4–8. Other tales include "Elves and the Shoemaker," "Talking Eggs," "Three Billy Goats Gruff," "Lon Po Po," and "Princess Furball." Available from Amazon.com and Barnes&Noble.com.

Somersaulter-Moats, prod. 1981. *Rapunzel.* Animated color film. 10 minutes. Ages 4–8. Faithful to the traditional tale. Distributed by Coronet/MTI Film and Video.

Free viewing on the Internet via Hulu: *Shelley Duvall's Faerie Tale Theatre,* http://www.hulu.com/watch/112369/shelley-duvalls-faerie-tale-theatre-rapunzel, running time 51:23, ages 4–8.

Rapunzel: The Books

Berenzy, Alix. 1998. *Rapunzel.* New York: Holt.

Bofill, Francesc. 2006. *Rapunzel.* Illustrated by Joma. San Francisco: Chronicle Books.

Ceccoli, Nicoletta. 2001. *Rapunzel.* Worthington, OH: Brighter Child.

Cech, John. 2010. *Rapunzel.* Illustrated by Fiona Sansom. New York: Sterling.

Dokey, Cameron. 2007. *Golden: A Retelling of "Rapunzel."* Illustrated by Mahlon F. Craft. New York: Simon Pulse.

Duntze, Dorothée. 2005. *Rapunzel.* New York: North-South.

Hood, Judy. 2008. *Rapunzel.* [Created and performed in American Sign Language.] Portland, OR: ASL Tales.

Isadora, Rachel. 2008. *Rapunzel.* New York: G.P. Putnam's Sons.

Jones, Christianne C. 2005. *Rapunzel.* Illustrated by Amy Bailey Muehlenhardt. Mankato, MN: Picture Window Books.

Lavreys, Debbie. 2010. *Rapunzel.* New York: Clavis Publications.

McCafferty, Catherine. 2002. *Rapunzel.* Worthington, OH: Brighter Child.

Roberts, Lynn, and David Roberts. 2003. *Rapunzel: A Groovy Fairy Tale.* New York: Abrams.

Smiley, Ben. 2010. *Tangled.* Illustrated by Victoria Ying. White Plains, NY: Golden/Disney.

Storace, Patricia. 2007. *Sugar Cane: A Caribbean Rapunzel.* Illustrated by Raul Colon. New York: Jump at the Sun/Hyperion Books for Children.

Zelinsky, Paul O. 2002. *Rapunzel.* New York: Dutton.

Rapunzel: I HAVE, WHO HAS Game

Directions: Cut all the cards apart. Each player gets one card. Begin with the question preceded by an asterisk (*). The student with the answer card responds.

I HAVE: The prince found Rapunzel and her tears restored his sight. *WHO HAS: What favor did the wife who was expecting a child ask her husband?	I HAVE: The witch climbed up Rapunzel's hair. WHO HAS: How did the prince discover Rapunzel?
I HAVE: She asked for lettuce from the garden next door. WHO HAS: Who caught the husband picking the lettuce?	I HAVE: He heard her singing and saw the witch climb up her hair. WHO HAS: What did the prince do when the witch left?
I HAVE: The witch who owned the garden caught the husband picking lettuce. WHO HAS: How did the husband escape punishment from the witch?	I HAVE: He climbed up Rapunzel's hair and asked her to marry him. WHO HAS: What did the witch do when she discovered the prince's visits to Rapunzel?
I HAVE: He promised her their first-born child. WHO HAS: What happened when the child was born?	I HAVE: She cut off Rapunzel's hair and hid her in the desert. WHO HAS: What happened to the prince?
I HAVE: The witch took the child away and shut her up in a tower with no door. WHO HAS: How did the witch visit Rapunzel and bring her food?	I HAVE: The prince was blinded and wandered the land for years searching for Rapunzel. WHO HAS: How did the story end?

Rapunzel: Library Treasure Hunt

Go to the children's nonfiction shelves. Look for each number on the spine of the books. What is each book about? That is the missing word. Write it on the line after the number. The player who finds all of the missing words first is the winner.

1. A woman asked her husband to bring her lettuce from a 635. _____	2. Rapunzel was locked up in a tower in the 577.3. _____
3. Rapunzel was shut up in the tower by a 133.4. _____	4. The witch climbed up Rapunzel's hair to bring her food and 391. _____
5. The prince heard Rapunzel's 782.42. _____	6. The witch hid Rapunzel in the 577.5. _____

_____

Key: 1. garden; 2. forest; 3. witch; 4. clothing; 5. song; 6. desert

Rapunzel: Word Search

L	E	Z	N	U	P	A	R
W	H	A	I	R	L	A	T
S	I	A	I	O	I	O	C
R	H	N	R	O	W	W	N
A	C	R	D	E	S	I	I
E	S	N	R	O	H	T	G
T	P	I	N	E	W	C	A
N	H	G	S	E	C	H	R

Words to find:

Rapunzel	witch	tower
hair	prince	song
window	thorns	tears

Rumpelstiltskin

(The following can also be done orally, with the children raising their hands to respond.)

Find Someone Who!

Discover what your group has in common with the characters and places in *Rumpelstiltskin*. Find a different name from the class or group for each item. The winner is the first to complete all eight items. The winner will then read each item and the person whose name is on each line will stand to verify that he or she can actually qualify for the item.

Find someone who . . .

1. Has made a promise. _____

2. Is a first-born child in the family. _____

3. Knows another word for DWARF. _____

4. Can write a five-word sentence with
   each word beginning with the letter R. _____

5. Can name an animal that eats straw. _____

6. Can name a character who built a house
   of straw. _____

7. Has played a guessing game. _____

8. Has a necklace with one or more pearls. _____

Storyteller's Introduction to *Rumpelstiltskin*

Put the cards on the next page on transparencies or on a chart large enough for the audience to read. The audience will respond when the storyteller raises a corresponding card with the verse number.

Storyteller:
A giant lie
The miller told.
His girl could spin
The straw to gold.
When hearing this
The king was thrilled
But if she failed
She would be killed.

Audience (1):
A giant lie
The miller told.
His girl could NOT
Spin straw to gold.

Storyteller:
Left alone
Amid her fears
The young girl filled
The room with tears.
If, come morning,
Gold was seen
The girl would then
Become the queen.
BUT . . .

Audience (1):
A giant lie
The miller told.
His girl could NOT
Spin straw to gold.

Storyteller:
Then who appeared?
A little man.
"Stop your tears,
The task I can
Easily perform for you
However a reward is due.
"I know!" he said,
Then he smiled.

"You must give me
Your first-born child."
She promised him
The story's told
Then he spun
The straw to gold.
A year went by
The new queen smiled
In her arms
Was an infant child.
The dwarf appeared
Said, "Guess my name,
Or the child
I shall claim."
A messenger went
Far and near
Then came the day
He would hear
A dwarf who danced
And sang out loud
His secret name
For he was proud.

Audience (2):
Rumpelstiltskin was so proud
He danced and sang
His name aloud.

Storyteller:
The messenger told the queen
Of the dwarf
He had seen.
Now it was that
She could claim
RUMPELSTILTSKIN was his name.

Audience (3):
Ghosts and goblins,
Trolls and witches,
He was just too proud
For his britches.

(1)

A giant lie
the miller told.
His girl could NOT
Spin straw to gold.

(2)

Rumpelstiltskin was
so proud
He danced and said
his name aloud.

(3)

Ghosts and goblins,
Trolls and witches,
He was just too proud
For his britches.

Rumpelstiltskin: The Films

Campbell, Hugh, prod. 1985. *Rumpelstiltskin*. Narrated by Christopher Plummer. Animated color film. 30 minutes. Ages 4–8. Follows the original story line. Distributed by Family Home Entertainment.

Duvall, Shelley, prod. 1982. *Rumpelstiltskin*. Faerie Tale Theatre. Starring Shelley Duvall, Hervé Villachaize, Ned Beatty. Live action color film. 60 minutes. Ages 6–adult. Departs from the original in that the queen rather than the messenger discovers the name. Distributed by Fox Video.

Hanna-Barbera and Hallmark, prods. 1990. *Rumpelstiltskin*. Narrated by Olivia Newton-John. Animated color film. 30 minutes. Ages 4–8. Less grim than other versions and includes musical numbers. Distributed by Hanna-Barbera Home Video.

MGM, prod. 2005. *Rumpelstiltskin*. Starring Amy Irving, Billy Barty, Priscilla Pointer. Live action color musical. 84 minutes. Ages 4–adult. Follows the original story line. Distributed by MGM Home Video. Available from Amazon.com.

Perspective Films, prod. 1981. *Rumpelstiltskin*. Animated color film. 12 minutes. Ages 5–10. Faithful to the original tale. Distributed by Coronet/MTI Film and Video.

Free viewing on the Internet via YouTube: *Rumpelstiltskin*, http://www.youtube.com/watch?v=f6bwyILxtYA, running time 5:35, ages 4–8.

Rumpelstiltskin: The Books

Ainsworth, Ruth. 1980. *Rumpelstiltskin*. London: Purnell.

Amery, Heather. 2006. *Rumpelstiltskin*. Usborne Fairytale Sticker Stories. London: Usborne.

Arengo, Sue, and Gianluca Garofalo. 2004. *Rumpelstiltskin*. New York: Oxford University Press.

Cooley, Gary. 1992. *Rumpelstiltskin*. Kansas City, MO: Andrews McMeel.

Galdone, Paul. 1985. *Rumpelstiltskin*. New York: Houghton-Mifflin.

Mayo, Margaret, and Selina Young. 2003. *Rumpelstiltskin*. Illustrated by Philip Norman. London: Orchard.

Noel, Christopher. 2005. *Rumpelstiltskin*. Rabbit Ears Classic Tale. Illustrated by Peter Sis. Madison, NC: Spotlight.

Tarcov, Edith H. 1974. *Rumpelstiltskin: A Tale Told Long Ago*. Illustrated by Edward Gorey. New York: Four Winds Press.

Zelinsky, Paul O. 1986. *Rumpelstiltskin*. New York: Dutton.

Rumpelstiltskin: I HAVE, WHO HAS Game

Directions: Cut all the cards apart. Each player gets one card. Begin with the question preceded by an asterisk (*). The student with the answer card responds.

I HAVE: The queen guessed his name and was able to keep her child. *WHO HAS: What did the bragging miller tell the king?	I HAVE: The second night she gave the dwarf a ring. WHO HAS: What gift did she promise on the third night?
I HAVE: The miller said his daughter could spin straw into gold. WHO HAS: What was the punishment if she could not spin straw into gold?	I HAVE: If she became queen, she promised her first-born child. WHO HAS: What happened a year later when the dwarf came to claim the child?
I HAVE: The girl would lose her life. WHO HAS: What was the reward if she could spin straw into gold?	I HAVE: The queen was given three days to guess the dwarf's name. WHO HAS: What did the queen do to find out the dwarf's name?
I HAVE: The reward was that she could become queen. WHO HAS: Who helped the girl?	I HAVE: The queen sent messengers throughout the land searching for names. WHO HAS: What did the queen's messenger find?
I HAVE: A small dwarf helped the girl in exchange for her necklace on the first night. WHO HAS: What payment did she give the dwarf on the second night?	I HAVE: The messenger found a little man bragging that his name was Rumpelstiltskin. WHO HAS: What happened on the third night when the dwarf appeared?

Rumpelstiltskin: Library Treasure Hunt

Go to the children's nonfiction shelves. Look for each number on the spine of the books. What is each book about? That is the missing word. Write it on the line after the number. The player who finds all of the missing words first is the winner.

1. The miller made a trip to the king's 728.8. _____	2. To spin straw into gold, the girl needed 793.8. _____
3. The first two nights she gave the dwarf her 745.58. _____	4. To the greedy king, lots of gold meant lots of 332.4. _____
5. If she lost her child, the queen would have a broken 612.1. _____	6. The queen's messenger heard the dwarf singing a 782.42. _____

_____

Key: 1. castle; 2. magic; 3. jewels; 4. money; 5. heart; 6. song

Rumpelstiltskin: Word Search

R	E	T	H	G	U	A	D
I	C	S	T	R	A	W	G
N	A	N	E	E	A	D	K
G	L	U	Q	R	I	E	L
E	K	G	F	U	A	Q	E
W	C	O	N	R	E	L	C
R	E	L	L	I	M	E	E
I	N	D	F	N	K	A	N

Words to find:

miller	daughter	dwarf
king	straw	gold
necklace	ring	queen

The Seven Ravens

(The following can also be done orally, with the children raising their hands to respond.)

Find Someone Who!

Discover what your group has in common with the characters and places in *The Seven Ravens*. Find a different name in the class or group for each item. The winner is the first to complete all eight items. The winner will then read each item and the person whose name is on each line will stand to verify that he or she can actually qualify for the item.

Find someone who . . .

1. Has seven children in his or her family. _____

2. Can name a story with a magic spell. _____

3. Has kept a secret. _____

4. Has gone on a long trip. _____

5. Has done something nice for a brother or sister. _____

6. Can name something that flutters. _____

7. Can say a word that rhymes with GIRL. _____

8. Knows what a cloak is. _____

Storyteller's Introduction to *The Seven Ravens*

Story Summary:

A man sent his seven sons to a well for water for their ill sister. Dropping the water jug in the well, they were afraid to return. When they did not return home, the father wished that the boys would become ravens and his wish was granted.

When their little sister grew up and learned about the enchantment, she set off to find her brothers, taking with her only bread, water, and a small chair. She visited the sun, the moon, and the stars and at last came to a glass mountain that she opened by putting her little finger in the door.

She met a dwarf who led her to the place where the ravens dined. She took a sip from each cup and in the last cup dropped the ring she had brought with her. She ate off of each plate, breaking the spell and the ravens once again become her brothers.

Directions:

Distribute one story strip (see next page) to each of ten children. Challenge the group to line them up in an order they believe will tell the story. When they are done, each child reads his or her strip.

After hearing the story or seeing the film, ask the group to repeat the line-up activity. Is the second line-up the same as the first? Why or why not?

(1) The angry father wished them to become ravens and got his wish.

(2) She met a dwarf and tasted food from the ravens' plates.

(3) The water jug fell into the well.

(4) She took with her bread, water, and a chair.

(5) The ravens became her brothers once again.

(6) Seven brothers went to get water for their new baby sister.

(7) She cut off her finger to open the Glass Mountain.

(8) As a young woman, the girl went to search for her brothers.

(9) The brothers were afraid to go home.

(10) She visited the sun, the moon, and the stars.

Key: 6, 3, 9, 1, 8, 4, 10, 7, 2, 5

The Seven Ravens: The Films

DEFA Studio, prod. 1971. *The Seven Ravens.* Animated color film. 21 minutes. Ages 5–8. Faithful to the original Grimm tale with a musical background. Distributed by Coronet/MTI Film and Video.

New World Video, prod. 1979. *The Brothers Grimm Fairy Tales.* Animated color film. 35 minutes. Ages 5–8. Faithful to the original Grimm tale; also includes "Little Red Riding Hood." Available from Amazon.com.

Free viewing on the Internet via Google: *Grimm Brothers Fairytale—The Seven Ravens,* http://video.google.com/videoplay?docid=6006646552227704165#, running time 21:00.

The Seven Ravens: The Books

The Complete Grimm's Fairy Tales. 2006. Introduction by Padraic Colum. New York: Pantheon.

Crawford, Elizabeth D., trans. 1981. *The Seven Ravens.* Illustrated by Lisbeth Zwerger. New York: Morrow.

Diamond, Donna. 1979. *The Seven Ravens.* New York: Viking.

Geringer, Laura. 1994. *The Seven Ravens.* Illustrated by Edward Gazsi. New York: HarperCollins.

Lucas, E.V., Lucy Crane, and Marian Edward, trans. 2008. *Grimms' Fairy Tales.* New York: Grosset and Dunlap.

Pirotta, Saviour. 2006. *The McElderry Book of Grimms' Fairy Tales.* Illustrated by Emma Chichester Clark. New York: Margaret K. McElderry.

Rackham, Arthur, illus. 2001. *Grimm's Fairy Tales.* New York: Seastar Books.

The Seven Ravens: I HAVE, WHO HAS Game

Directions: Cut all the cards apart. Each player gets one card. Begin with the question preceded by an asterisk (*). The student with the answer card responds.

I HAVE: The seven ravens became human once again. *WHO HAS: What joyous event happened to a couple with seven sons?	I HAVE: She went to seek her brothers. WHO HAS: What happened when she visited the stars?
I HAVE: The wife gave birth to a daughter. WHO HAS: What task did the father give to the seven sons?	I HAVE: The stars gave her a drumstick to use to open the way through the Glass Mountain. WHO HAS: What happened when she lost the drumstick?
I HAVE: The sons were to bring water to their new sister's baptism. WHO HAS: What happened when the sons went to get water?	I HAVE: She cut off her finger and opened a door with it. WHO HAS: Who did she meet inside the mountain?
I HAVE: They dropped the jug in the well and were too afraid to go home. WHO HAS: What did the father do when the sons did not return home?	I HAVE: She met a dwarf and ate from her brothers' plates. WHO HAS: What happened when the seven ravens returned?
I HAVE: The father got his wish that they become ravens. WHO HAS: What did the girl do when she became a young woman?	I HAVE: One raven found a ring in his glass put there by his sister. WHO HAS: What magic did the ring bring about?

The Seven Ravens: Library Treasure Hunt

Go to the children's nonfiction shelves. Look for each number on the spine of the books. What is each book about? That is the missing word. Write it on the line after the number. The player who finds all of the missing words first is the winner.

1. Seven sons went to get 363.6 for their new sister. _____	2. The angry father turned his sons into seven 598s. _____
3. For her journey, the girl took water, a chair, and some 641.8. _____	4. The girl visited the moon and the 525. _____
5. The 523.8 gave her a drumstick. _____	6. She was to use the drumstick to open the glass 551.4. _____

Key: 1. water; 2. birds; 3. bread; 4. sun; 5. stars; 6. mountain

The Seven Ravens: Word Search

S	R	A	T	S	S	S	A
W	A	T	E	R	N	U	E
R	R	C	A	E	O	N	H
G	D	H	V	H	M	R	H
N	N	A	N	T	G	G	A
R	R	I	E	O	R	W	S
R	U	R	R	R	O	R	O
O	S	S	B	B	B	M	E

Words to find:

ravens	brothers	ring
water	bread	chair
sun	moon	stars

Sleeping Beauty

(The following can also be done orally, with the children raising their hands to respond.)

Find Someone Who!

Discover what your group has in common with the characters and places in *Sleeping Beauty*. Find a different name in the class or group for each item. The winner is the first to complete all eight items. The winner will then read each item and the person whose name is on each line will stand to verify that he or she can actually qualify for the item.

Find someone who . . .

1. Knows what a spindle is. _____

2. Has a godmother. _____

3. Can count to 100 by tens. _____

4. Knows what the word "enchantment" means. _____

5. Was late to school because he or she overslept. _____

6. Has pricked his or her finger on a thorn. _____

7. Can say a word that rhymes with SLEEP. _____

8. Can name two castle workers and their jobs. _____

Storyteller's Introduction to *Sleeping Beauty*

At a signal from the storyteller, **audience members repeat the lines in bold print**.

A princess was born
To a king and queen.
A party was given
That she might be seen.
Eleven gifts bestowed
By twelve witches wise
Then a thirteenth appeared
With an awful surprise.

In her fifteenth year
The princess would feel
A prick on her finger
From a spinning wheel.
The cut will not mend
The cut will, instead,
Cause the sweet princess
To fall down quite dead.

"But wait," said witch twelve.
"Put aside all your tears.
Instead of her death
She'll sleep one hundred years."
The maiden grew up,
So lovely and sweet,
Till at age fifteen
A woman she'd meet,
Spinning away
At a wheel more and more,
Then the girl pricked her finger
And fell to the floor.

Upon the whole castle
The queen and the king,
The horses, the dogs,
And each living thing
Fell asleep like the princess
From dusk to daybreak,
Till 100 years passed
No one was awake.

Now 100 years later.
Early one morn
A young prince was caught
In a hedge by a thorn.
He'd heard of the princess,
The long-sleeping lass,
So through the thorn hedge
He determined to pass.

The curse would be up
In a matter of hours.
The thorns disappeared
And turned into flowers.
The young man approached
The castle so still.
He searched for the princess
All over until
He found her asleep,
The lovely young miss.
He touched her soft lips
And gave her a kiss.

The princess awakened
From her long repose,
And after that kiss
From her sleep she arose,
And throughout the castle
Awakened were all
The horses, the dogs,
The flies on the wall.
Then a wedding was held
With the prince and his bride
They both said I DO!
As they stood side by side.

Sleeping Beauty: The Films

Alexovich, David, prod. 1990. *Sleeping Beauty*. Animated full-color film. 12 minutes. Ages 6–10. Very different from the original tale. Distributed by Britannica.

Duvall, Shelley, prod. 1983. *Sleeping Beauty*. Faerie Tale Theatre. Starring Bernadette Peters, Beverly DeAngelo, Christopher Reeve, Sally Kellerman. Live action color film. 60 minutes. Ages 10–adult. Follows the original tale closely. Laser disc version distributed by Image Entertainment.

Golban Globus Productions, prod. 1989. *Sleeping Beauty*. Starring Morgan Fairchild. Live action color film. 90 minutes. Ages 6–12. Fairly close to the original tale with some material added. Distributed by Cannon Video.

Halas and Batchelor, prod. 1969. *Sleeping Beauty*. Color film with some animation. 7 minutes. Ages 4–8. Quite different from the original story. Distributed by Britannica.

Jetlag Productions, prod. 1995. *Sleeping Beauty*. Voices of Tony Ail, Nathan Aswell, Chera Bailey, Kathleen Barr. Animated full-color film. 48 minutes. Ages 4–8. Follows the original tale. Distributed by Good Times Entertainment.

Walt Disney, prod. 1959. *Sleeping Beauty*. Animated full-color film. 75 minutes. Ages 4–8. With music from Tchaikovsky's ballet. Distributed by Buena Vista Home Video.

Free viewing on the Internet via YouTube: *Sleeping Beauty*, http://www.youtube.com/watch?v=DVM_481ZPV4, running time 4:00.

Sleeping Beauty: The Books

Blair, Eric. 2005. *Sleeping Beauty*. Illustrated by Todd Ouren. Mankato, MN: Picture Window Books.

Craft, Mahlon F. 2002. *Sleeping Beauty*. Illustrated by K. Y. Craft. New York: SeaStar Books.

Desclot, Miquel. 2003. *Sleeping Beauty*. San Francisco: Chronicle Books.

Geras, Adele. 2004. *Sleeping Beauty*. Illustrated by Christian Birmingham. London: Orchard.

Hapka, Catherine. 2008. *Walt Disney's Sleeping Beauty*. New York: Random House.

Hyman, Trina Schart. 1977. *Sleeping Beauty: From the Brothers Grimm*. New York: Little, Brown and Company.

Mass, Wendy. 2009. *Sleeping Beauty: The One Who Took the Really Long Nap*. New York: Scholastic.

San Jose, Christine. 1997. *Sleeping Beauty*. Honesdale, PA: Boyds Mills Press.

Wallner, John, and Peter Seymour. 1987. *Sleeping Beauty*. New York: Viking.

Sleeping Beauty: I HAVE, WHO HAS Game

Directions: Cut all the cards apart. Each player gets one card. Begin with the question preceded by an asterisk (*). The student with the answer card responds.

I HAVE: The prince and princess were married. *WHO HAS: What joyous event celebrated the birth of the princess?	I HAVE: Instead of death the princess would have a one-hundred-year sleep. WHO HAS: What happened when the princess pricked her finger on a spinning wheel?
I HAVE: The king gave a feast to celebrate his daughter's birth. WHO HAS: Who did the king invite to the feast?	I HAVE: The princess, king, and queen and all living things in the castle went to sleep for one hundred years. WHO HAS: Who approached the castle but was stopped by a thorn hedge?
I HAVE: The king invited twelve wise women to the feast. WHO HAS: What kind of gifts did the wise women give the child?	I HAVE: A prince approached the castle and entered the thorn hedge. WHO HAS: Why was the prince not injured by the thorns?
I HAVE: The wise women gave gifts of virtue, beauty, and riches. WHO HAS: What did the thirteenth woman who had not been invited give?	I HAVE: The thorns turned into flowers. WHO HAS: What happened when the prince found Sleeping Beauty?
I HAVE: The thirteenth woman told of the death of the princess at age fifteen from pricking her finger on a spinning wheel. WHO HAS: How did another woman change the prediction?	I HAVE: The prince kissed her and she awakened along with everyone in the castle. WHO HAS: How did the story end?

Sleeping Beauty: Library Treasure Hunt

Go to the children's nonfiction shelves. Look for each number on the spine of the books. What is each book about? That is the missing word. Write it on the line after the number. The player who finds all of the missing words first is the winner.

1. A 133.4 declared that the girl would sleep for one hundred years. _____	2. Spinning wheels were banned from the 728.8. _____
3. The whole castle fell asleep, including the 636.7. _____	4. The prince arrived at the castle on a 636.1. _____
5. The sharp thorns turned into 582.13. _____	6. The story ended with a 392. _____

Key: 1. witch; 2. castle; 3. dogs; 4. horse; 5. flowers; 6. wedding

Sleeping Beauty: Word Search

P	O	I	S	Q	P	A	D	N
R	D	K	F	G	E	U	S	N
O	N	E	I	A	S	P	N	E
S	S	E	C	N	I	R	P	S
E	E	K	I	N	G	R	S	M
B	P	E	D	E	I	D	Y	E
U	S	L	E	E	P	R	O	E
D	E	R	I	U	E	O	P	M
P	I	R	E	Q	A	B	B	I

Words to find:

king	queen	princess
prince	fairy	spindle
rosebud	sleep	kingdom

Snow White and the Seven Dwarfs

(The following can also be done orally, with the children raising their hands to respond.)

Find Someone Who!

Discover what your group has in common with the characters and places in *Snow White and the Seven Dwarfs*. Find a different name in the class or group for each item. The winner is the first to complete all eight items. The winner will then read each item and the person whose name is on each line will stand to verify that he or she can actually qualify for the item.

Find someone who . . .

1. Has a first name that begins with the letter S. _____

2. Can name a fairy tale with a wicked queen. _____

3. Has walked in the woods. _____

4. Knows what a dwarf is. _____

5. Likes apples best of all fruits. _____

6. Can name seven jobs to do around the house. _____

7. Can say a word that rhymes with WHITE. _____

8. Has seen the movie *Snow White.* _____

Storyteller's Introduction to *Snow White and the Seven Dwarfs*

At a signal from the storyteller, **children will repeat the last lines of each verse.**

Little Snow White
Lost her dear mother,
Then her father, the king,
Married another
Who touched a mirror
With her evil hand.
It told her Snow White
Was fairest in the land.

A hunter she summoned
And to him she said,
"Take Snow White
In the woods
And leave her there dead."
But once in the woods,
The hunter said, "Flee!"
The hunter was kind
He let her go free.

She ran through the woods
As quick as a mouse
Till she came upon
A cozy small house.
She opened the door,
Walked in, and then
Found herself staring
At seven small men.

Meanwhile back at
The palace so grand,
The queen touched the mirror
With her clawlike hand.

It told her Snow White
Was alive in the wood,
So the Queen went to find her
As fast as she could.

With a black cloak that covered
All but her eyes,
She knocked on the door
In her beggar's disguise
And offered an apple
Held in her hand
To poison Snow White,
Fairest in all the land.

The girl bit the apple
and fell to the floor.
The Queen disappeared
and was seen no more.
The dwarves moaned quite loudly,
they sobbed and they cried,
As they carried Snow White
To a bier outside.

Along came a prince
Who saw the sweet miss,
Leaned over the bier,
And gave her a kiss,
And asked him to join her
In a royal life.
Snow White and the prince
Then became man and wife.

Snow White and the Seven Dwarfs: The Films

Csupo, Gabor, and Arlene Klasky, prods. 2005. *RugRats: Tales from the Crib: Snow White*. Voices of Amanda Bynes, Kenan Thompson, Jeffrey Licon. Animated full-color film. 119 minutes. Ages 4–9. Close retelling of the original tale using Rugrats as the dwarfs. Distributed by Paramount Home Entertainment.

Duvall, Shelley, prod. 1983. *Snow White and the Seven Dwarfs*. Faerie Tale Theatre. Starring Elizabeth McGovern, Vincent Price, Vanessa Redgrave. Live action full-color film. 53 minutes. Ages 6–adult. Faithful to the original tale with minor changes. Distributed by Fox Video.

Golan-Globus Productions, prod. 1989. *Snow White*. Starring Diana Rigg, Billy Barty. Live action color film. 85 minutes. Ages 6–adult. A musical version that follows the original tale. Distributed by Cannon Video.

Rankin-Bass, prod. 1989. *Snow White*. Animated color film. 26 minutes. Ages 6–10. A highly condensed version of the story. Distributed by Lucerne Media.

Shami, Aria, and Bob Shami, prods. 2006. *Snow White and the Seven Dwarfs*. Animated full-color film. 25 minutes. Ages 4–8. Text included. Available on DVD. Distributed by Shami Productions.

Walt Disney, prod. 1937. *Snow White and the Seven Dwarfs*. Voices of Adriana Caselotti, Lucille LaVerne, Pinto Colvig, Roy Atwell. Animated full-color film. 83 minutes. Ages 5–adult. A musical version that follows the original tale. Distributed by Paramount Home Video.

Free viewing on the Internet via YouTube: *Snow White*, http://www.youtube.com/watch ?v=Bh9_UncKFUM, running time 8:34.

Snow White and the Seven Dwarfs: The Books

Aiken, Joan. 2002. *Snow White and the Seven Dwarfs*. Illustrated by Belinda Downes. New York: DK Publishing.

Cooper, Melinda. 2005. *Snow White*. New York: Dutton Children's Books.

Gag, Wanda. 2004. *Snow White and the Seven Dwarfs*. Minneapolis: University of Minnesota Press.

Gréban, Quentin. 2009. *Snow White*. New York: North-South.

Heins, Paul, trans. 1974. *Snow White*. Illustrated by Trina Schart Hyman. New York: Little, Brown and Company.

Jarrell, Randall. 1972. *Snow White and the Seven Dwarfs*. Illustrated by Nancy Ekholm Burkert. New York: Farrar, Straus, & Giroux.

Ljungkvist, Laura. 2003. *Snow White and the Seven Dwarfs*. New York: Abrams.

Rylant, Cynthia. 2009. *Walt Disney's Snow White and the Seven Dwarfs*. White Plains, NY: Disney Press.

Santore, Charles. 2010. *Snow White*. New York: Sterling.

Torres, Melissa A. 2003. *Snow White*. Illustrated by Barbara Lanza. New York: Scholastic.

Snow White and the Seven Dwarfs: I HAVE, WHO HAS Game

Directions: Cut all the cards apart. Each player gets one card. Begin with the question preceded by an asterisk (*). The student with the answer card responds.

I HAVE: A prince's kiss brought Snow White back to life. *WHO HAS: What happened to Snow White's mother?	I HAVE: Everything was very small and very clean. WHO HAS: Who lived in the little house?
I HAVE: Snow White's mother died and her father, the king, remarried. WHO HAS: What kind of woman was Snow White's stepmother?	I HAVE: Seven dwarfs lived in the house and found Snow White asleep there. WHO HAS: What did the dwarfs ask Snow White to do?
I HAVE: Snow White's stepmother was an evil, jealous woman. WHO HAS: Why did the stepmother order the woodsman to kill Snow White?	I HAVE: She was to cook, clean, make beds, sew, and knit in order to stay and want for nothing. WHO HAS: How did the wicked queen discover that Snow White was still alive?
I HAVE: She was jealous when the mirror said Snow White was the fairest in the land. WHO HAS: What happened when the woodsman took Snow White into the woods?	I HAVE: The magic mirror told the queen Snow White was alive. WHO HAS: What did the queen do when she found Snow White was alive?
I HAVE: The woodsman let the girl go. WHO HAS: What did she find in the little house in the woods?	I HAVE: She gave her a poisoned apple, so she appeared to be dead. WHO HAS: What brought Snow White back to life?

Snow White and the Seven Dwarfs: Library Treasure Hunt

Go to the children's nonfiction shelves. Look for each number on the spine of the books. What is each book about? That is the missing word. Write it on the line after the number. The player who finds all of the missing words first is the winner.

1. Snow White lived in a 728.8 with her father and stepmother. _____	2. The wicked stepmother had a 793.8 mirror. _____
3. The stepmother told the woods-man to take Snow White to the 577.3. _____	4. Snow White became a member of the dwarf 306.8. _____
5. The wicked woman gave Snow White a poisoned 634. _____	6. The dwarfs thought the apple caused Snow White's 155.9. _____

Key: 1. castle; 2. magic; 3. forest; 4. family; 5. apple; 6. death

Snow White and the Seven Dwarfs: Word Search

R	D	S	N	N	P	N	C	D
F	A	P	P	L	E	A	O	W
S	W	P	F	E	E	M	F	A
W	D	W	U	C	L	S	F	R
F	E	Q	N	A	S	D	I	F
E	T	I	H	W	W	O	N	S
W	R	T	S	E	R	O	F	S
P	A	R	R	E	N	W	R	A
S	P	O	R	A	O	E	E	O

Words to find:

Snow White	queen	woodsman
prince	dwarfs	apple
forest	sleep	coffin

The Stonecutter

(The following can also be done orally, with the children raising their hands to respond.)

Find Someone Who!

Discover what your group has in common with the characters and places in *The Stonecutter*. Find a different name in the class or group for each item. The winner is the first to complete all eight items. The winner will then read each item and the person whose name is on each line will stand to verify that he or she can actually qualify for the item.

Find someone who . . .

1. Can find Japan on a map.   _____

2. Name one use for a wagon full of small stones.   _____

3. Can name something good the sun does.   _____

4. Can name something good the rain does.   _____

5. Has climbed a mountain.   _____

6. Has a first name that begins with the letter T.   _____

7. Can say a word that rhymes with MOUNTAIN.   _____

8. Has made a wish that came true.   _____

Storyteller's Introduction to *The Stonecutter*

When the storyteller points up with his or her hand, the audience responds with "That's good!"

Storyteller: There was once a poor stonecutter who spent his days chipping away stone at the base of a mountain. At the end of each day he would take his cart of stone to town to sell. One morning he is chipping away when he stops for a prince who is riding by. Soldiers walk before him and dancers follow him. The Stonecutter asks the Great Spirit to let him become a prince and he gets his wish.

Audience: That's good!

Storyteller: No, that was bad because the sun proved to be more powerful than the prince. It burned everything it touched and forced the prince to take off his robe. So the Stonecutter/Prince asked the Great Spirit to let him become the sun.

Audience: That's good!

Storyteller: No, that was bad because a cloud proved to be mightier than the sun. It blotted out the sun and rained so hard it flooded the land. So the Stonecutter/Prince/Sun asked the Great Spirit to let him become the cloud.

Audience: That's good!

Storyteller: No, that was bad because the rain from the cloud could not wash away the mountain. Since the mountain was most powerful of all, the Stonecutter/Prince/Sun/Cloud asked the Great Spirit to let him become the mountain.

Audience: That's good!

Storyteller: No, really it was bad because early the next morning a lonely Stonecutter was chipping away at the base of the mountain.

The Stonecutter: The Films

Maverick Entertainment, prod. 2007. *The Stonecutter*. Starring Tieki Pambrun, Papa Matarau, and Fenua. Live action color film. 80 minutes. Ages 6–adult. Deviates considerably from the traditional tale. Distributed by Maverick Entertainment.

McDermott, Gerald, and Weston Woods, prods. 1975. *The Stonecutter*. Animated color film. 6 minutes. Ages 4–10. Later to become a book, this version uses abstract art to tell the tale. Distributed by Weston Woods.

Van Deusen, Pieter, prod. 1988. *Folktales from Two Lands*. Animated color film. 17 minutes. Ages 5–9. Contains two tales, "The Fisherman and His Wife" and "The Stonecutter." Distributed by Churchill Media.

Free viewing on the Internet via You Tube: *The Stonecutter*, http://www .youtube.com/watch?v=mWt1CRvlfSs, running time 5:09.

The Stonecutter: The Books

Arnold, Francis M. 2010. *The Stonecutter: A Japanese Legend*. Illustrated by Elizabeth Harrison. Charleston, SC: Nabu Press.

Benton, Lynne. 2009. *The Stonecutter*. Illustrated by Lee Cosgrove. London: Usborne.

Demi. 1995. *The Stonecutter*. New York: Knopf.

Harney, Will. 2010. *The Stonecutter*. North Shore, MA: Harney Publishing.

Longoni, Alberto. 1971. *The Stonecutter*. Picture Story Books. London: Methuen Books.

McDermott, Gerald. 1975. *The Stonecutter*. New York: Penguin.

Muth, Jon J., and John Kuramoto. 2009. *The Stonecutter*. Illustrated by Jon J. Muth. New York: Feiwel and Friends.

Newton, Patricia. 1990. *The Stonecutter*. New York: Putnam.

Polette, Keith. 2009. *Moon Over the Mountain / Luna Sobre La Montana*. Illustrated by Michael Kress-Russick. McHenry, IL: Raven Tree Press.

The Stonecutter: I HAVE, WHO HAS Game

Directions: Cut all the cards apart. Each player gets one card. Begin with the question preceded by an asterisk (*). The student with the answer card responds.

I HAVE: A poor stonecutter began chipping away at the base of the mountain. *WHO HAS: How did the poor Japanese man make a living?	I HAVE: The Stonecutter asked the Great Spirit to let him become the sun. WHO HAS: What happened when the Stonecutter became the sun?
I HAVE: The poor man chipped away the stone from the mountain and then he sold it in the city. WHO HAS: What did the Stonecutter see passing by?	I HAVE: He burned up the grass and flowers and forced people to remove their cloaks. WHO HAS: What proved to be more powerful than the sun?
I HAVE: He saw soldiers, dancers, and a prince. WHO HAS: What did he ask the Great Spirit to do?	I HAVE: A cloud with heavy rain was more powerful than the sun. WHO HAS: What was more powerful than the cloud?
I HAVE: The Stonecutter asked the Great Spirit to let him become a prince. WHO HAS: What happened when the stonecutter's wish was granted?	I HAVE: The mountain was more powerful since the rain could not wash it away. WHO HAS: What was the Stonecutter's last wish?
I HAVE: He became a prince but found the sun was more powerful than he, as it forced him to take off his cloak. WHO HAS: What was the Stonecutter's second request to the Great Spirit?	I HAVE: The Stonecutter's last wish was to become the mountain. WHO HAS: What happened when he became the mountain?

The Stonecutter: Library Treasure Hunt

Go to the children's nonfiction shelves. Look for each number on the spine of the books. What is each book about? That is the missing word. Write it on the line after the number. The player who finds all of the missing words first is the winner.

1. The story of the Stonecutter takes place in 952. _____	2. The hot sun forced the prince to remove his 391. _____
3. The Stonecutter asked the Spirit to let him become the 525. _____	4. The 551.57 was more powerful than the sun. _____
5. The rain from the cloud caused a 551.48. _____	6. The 551.4 was the most powerful of all. _____

Key: 1. Japan; 2. clothing; 3. sun; 4. cloud; 5. flood; 6. mountain

The Stonecutter: Word Search

A	C	L	O	U	D	S	I
N	I	A	T	N	U	O	M
T	E	E	I	N	E	L	I
I	U	J	C	R	U	D	O
R	I	A	T	N	M	I	S
I	U	P	U	C	I	E	U
P	D	A	N	C	E	R	S
S	E	N	O	T	S	S	P

Words to find:

Japan	prince	sun
clouds	soldier	mountain
dancers	spirit	stones

The Three Little Pigs

(The following can also be done orally, with the children raising their hands to respond.)

Find Someone Who!

Discover what your group has in common with the characters and places in *The Three Little Pigs*. Find a different name in the class or group for each item. The winner is the first to complete all eight items. The winner will then read each item and the person whose name is on each line will stand to verify that he or she can actually qualify for the item.

Find someone who . . .

1. Can name a fairy tale with a wolf. _____

2. Has moved into a new house. _____

3. Can name something you can make with sticks. _____

4. Knows what the word "famished" means. _____

5. Has played a trick on someone. _____

6. Knows what pigs eat. _____

7. Can say a word that rhymes with BRICKS. _____

8. Has two brothers. _____

Storyteller's Introduction to *The Three Little Pigs*

Divide the children into two groups. At a signal from the storyteller, one group, the wolf, says, "Little Pig, little pig, let me come in." The second group, the pig, answers, "Not by the hair of my chinny chin chin." The first group, the wolf, then says, "Then I'll huff and I'll puff and I'll blow your house in."

Storyteller: Three pigs set out to build their houses. The first pig met a man who gave him some straw. He built his straw house and was having his tea when a wolf knocked on the door.

Wolf: Little Pig, little pig, let me come in.

Pig: Not by the hair of my chinny chin chin.

Wolf: Then I'll huff and I'll puff and I'll blow your house in.

Storyteller: The wolf huffed and he puffed and he blew the house in and ate up that little pig.

The second pig met a man who gave him some sticks. He built his stick house and was having his tea when a wolf knocked on the door.

Wolf: Little Pig, little pig, let me come in.

Pig: Not by the hair of my chinny chin chin.

Wolf: Then I'll huff and I'll puff and I'll blow your house in.

Storyteller: The wolf huffed and he puffed and he blew the house in and ate up that little pig.

The third pig met a man who gave him some bricks. He built his straw house and was having his tea when a wolf knocked on the door.

Wolf: Little Pig, little pig, let me come in.

Pig: Not by the hair of my chinny chin chin.

Wolf: Then I'll huff and I'll puff and I'll blow your house in.

Storyteller: The wolf huffed and he puffed but could not blow down the brick house.

He go so angry that he decided to catch the pig by climbing down the chimney. When the pig saw that, he hung a pot of water and made a blazing fire. Down came the wolf into the hot water.

Howling, he jumped out of the pot, ran out the door and was never seen again.

The Three Little Pigs: The Films

Duvall, Shelley, prod. 1985. *The Three Little Pigs.* Faerie Tale Theatre. Starring Billy Crystal, Jeff Goldblum, Valerie Perrine. Live action full-color film. 60 minutes. Ages 8–adult. Many details and characters added and the animals are given personalities. Distributed by Fox Video.

Rabbit Ears Productions, prod. 1989. *Three Billy Goats Gruff and the Three Little Pigs.* Narrated by Holly Hunter. Color film with limited animation. 30 minutes. Ages 4–8. Faithful retelling of both tales. Distributed by SVS/Triumph.

Walt Disney, prod. 1956. *The Three Little Pigs.* Animated full-color film. 9 minutes. Ages 4–10. Some differences between the film and book versions. Distributed by Coronet/MTI Film and Video.

Free viewing on the Internet via YouTube: *Three Little Pigs*, http://www.youtube .com/watch?v=qTAvkwuTUbM&feature=related, running time 5:16.

The Three Little Pigs: The Books

Galdone, Paul. 2001. *The Three Little Pigs.* New York: Clarion.

Gay, Mary Louise. 2004. *The Three Little Pigs.* Toronto: Groundwood Books.

Golden Books. 2004. *Three Little Pigs.* Little Golden Book. Racine, WI: Western Publishing.

Guarnaccia, Steven. 2010. *The Three Little Pigs: An Architectural Tale.* New York: Abrams.

Hillert, Margaret. 2007. *The Three Little Pigs.* Illustrated by Irma Wilde. Chicago: Norwood House Press.

Johnson, Richard. 2007. *Three Little Pigs.* Flip-Up Fairy Tales. Auburn, ME: Child's Play International.

Kellogg, Steven, illus. 2002. *The Three Little Pigs.* New York: HarperCollins.

Marshall, James. 1989. *The Three Little Pigs.* New York: Dial.

Moore, Maggie. 2003. *The Three Little Pigs.* Illustrated by Rob Hefferan. Mankato, MN: Picture Window Books.

Moser, Barry. 2001. *The Three Little Pigs.* New York: Little, Brown and Company.

Scieszka, Jon. 2001. *The True Story of the Three Little Pigs.* Illustrated by Lane Smith. New York: Puffin Books.

Seibert, Patricia. 2002. *The Three Little Pigs.* Worthington, OH: Brighter Child.

Wiesner, David, illus. 2001. *The Three Pigs.* New York: Clarion.

Zemach, Margot. 2009. *The Three Little Pigs.* New York: Farrar, Straus, and Giroux.

The Three Little Pigs: I HAVE, WHO HAS Game

Directions: Cut all the cards apart. Each player gets one card. Begin with the question preceded by an asterisk (*). The student with the answer card responds.

I HAVE: The wolf jumped out of the pot, ran away, and was never seen again. *WHO HAS: Why did the sow send the three pigs out to seek their fortune?	I HAVE: The second pig met a man with a bundle of sticks. WHO HAS: What did the man give the second pig?
I HAVE: The sow had no money to feed the three little pigs. WHO HAS: Who did the first pig meet?	I HAVE: The man gave the second pig enough sticks to build a house. WHO HAS: What happened to the second pig's house?
I HAVE: The first pig met a man with a load of straw. WHO HAS: What did the man with the load of straw do?	I HAVE: The wolf blew the house down and ate the second pig. WHO HAS: Who did third little pig meet?
I HAVE: The man gave the first pig straw to build a house. WHO HAS: How was the house of straw destroyed?	I HAVE: The third pig met a man who gave him bricks to build a house. WHO HAS: When the wolf could not blow down the brick house, what did he do?
I HAVE: The wolf blew the house down and ate up the first little pig. WHO HAS: Who did the second little pig meet?	I HAVE: The wolf fell down the chimney into a pot of boiling water. WHO HAS: What happened when the wolf landed in the boiling water?

The Three Little Pigs: Library Treasure Hunt

Go to the children's nonfiction shelves. Look for each number on the spine of the books. What is each book about? That is the missing word. Write it on the line after the number. The player who finds all of the missing words first is the winner.

1. This story is about three 636.4. _____	2. They each wanted to build a 690. _____
3. A 599.77 blew down the houses of straw and sticks. _____	4. The third pig planted 582.13 around his house. _____
5. The third pig built a 628.9 under the pot. _____	6. The wolf pretended he wanted a drink of 363.6. _____

_____

Key: 1. pigs; 2. house; 3. wolf; 4. flowers; 5. fire; 6. water

The Three Little Pigs: Word Search

K	S	T	I	C	K	S	C
T	O	N	W	O	T	U	E
T	K	S	A	O	S	T	S
W	W	S	W	K	E	S	U
O	R	A	C	P	R	O	O
L	L	I	R	O	O	F	H
F	R	S	R	T	F	C	W
B	S	P	I	G	S	C	F

Words to find:

pigs	house	bricks
sticks	straw	forest
town	wolf	cookpot

PART II

INTRODUCING HANS CHRISTIAN ANDERSEN

Hans Christian Andersen

Storyteller's Introduction

At a signal from the storyteller, thumbs up or thumbs down, the audience alternates responses by saying, "That's good!" and "That's bad!"

Storyteller: Hans Christian Andersen was born in Odense, Denmark, in 1805. His parents hoped he would some day be a successful businessman.

Audience: That's good!

Storyteller: No, that was bad because his very poor family lived in one room, there was little money for schooling, and Hans had to work in a tailor shop.

Audience: That's bad!

Storyteller: Not really, because Hans was a daydreamer and did poorly in school. He spent his time writing plays that came to the attention of Jonas Collin, a theatre director, who liked the plays.

Audience: That's good!

Storyteller: Hans didn't think so because Mr. Collin told the boy he needed more schooling, and he was treated badly and made fun of in school because of his strange appearance.

Audience: That's bad!

Storyteller: It was really good because Mr. Collin arranged for private lessons for Hans so that he was free to write his stories and plays.

Audience: That's good!

Storyteller: Yes, it was because his stories caught the attention of the King of Denmark, who gave Hans money that allowed him to travel widely and to write about his experiences, thus becoming a very famous author.

The Emperor's New Clothes

(The following can also be done orally, with the children raising their hands to respond.)

Find Someone Who!

Discover what your group has in common with the characters and places in *The Emperor's New Clothes*. Find a different name in the class or group for each item. The winner is the first to complete all eight items. The winner will then read each item and the person whose name is on each line will stand to verify that he or she can actually qualify for the item.

Find someone who . . .

1. Can name a fairy tale with a king. _____

2. In the past week has bought something to wear. _____

3. Has watched a parade. _____

4. Knows what the word "invisible" means. _____

5. Has played a trick on someone. _____

6. Knows what an emperor is. _____

7. Can say a word that rhymes with CLOTHES. _____

8. Has a younger brother or sister. _____

Storyteller's Introduction to *The Emperor's New Clothes*

Audience members say the lines in **bold print** at a signal from the storyteller.

An Emperor often
Struck a pose
Showing off
His elegant clothes.
Because he ruled
He had the power
To wear a new suit
Every hour.

As you can see
It's very plain
This Emperor
Was very vain.

One fateful day
Two strangers came
Made a most
Preposterous claim
A cloth they had
A work of art
Seen only by one
Really smart.
"Well," thought the Ruler
"I'm most astute
So make me up
A brand new suit."

As you can see
It's very plain
This Emperor
Was very vain.

And so within
The weaving rooms
The strangers worked
At empty looms.
The Emperor sent
His trusty aide
To see how well
The suit was made.
The aide saw nothing
How could this be?

He must not say
He could not see
He told the king
The suit was fine
An excellent cut
Superb design.
The strangers worked
From dusk till dawn
The suit was brought
To be tried on.
The Emperor blinked
How could this be?
He must not say
He could not see.
He tried it on
Then told his aide
He would lead
A grand parade.

As you can see
It's very plain
This Emperor
Was very vain.

The people saw nothing
How could this be?
They must not say
They could not see
Till a little child
Standing there
Said, "The Emperor's
Wearing his underwear."
The strangers left town
With the Emperor's gold
Leaving this age-old tale
To be told.

As you can see
It's very plain
This Emperor
Was very vain.

The Emperor's New Clothes: The Films

Duvall, Shelley, prod. 1986. *The Emperor's New Clothes*. Faerie Tale Theatre. Starring Alan Arkin, Art Carney, Dick Shawn. Live action color film. 60 minutes. Ages 8–12. True to the original tale except for the ending, when the impostors repent. Distributed by Fox Video.

Golan-Globus Productions, prod. 1989. *The Emperor's New Clothes*. Starring Sid Caesar, Robert Morse. Live action color film. 85 minutes. Ages 5–10. Some departure from the original tale but well done. Released on DVD 2005. Distributed by Cannon Video. Available from Amazon.com and Barnes&Noble.com.

Hanna-Barbera and Hallmark, prods. 1990. *The Emperor's New Clothes*. Timeless Tales. Voices of Olivia Newton-John, Dom De Luise. Animated color film. 30 minutes. Ages 4–8. Departs considerably from the original tale with animals in place of people. Distributed by Hanna-Barbera Home Video.

Weston Woods, prod. 1990. *The Emperor's New Clothes and Other Folktales*. Iconographic and animated color film. 30 minutes. Ages 4–8. Faithful retelling of the tale. Distributed by Children's Circle, Weston Woods.

Free viewing on the Internet via Hulu: *Emperor's New Clothes*, http://www.hulu.com/watch/112387/shelley-duvalls-faerie-tale-theatre-the-emperors-new-clothes, running time 54:42, and http://www.hulu.com/watch/137357/the-emperors-new-clothes, running time 1:23:00.

The Emperor's New Clothes: The Books

Andersen, Hans Christian. 2000. *The Emperor's New Clothes: An All-Star Illustrated Retelling of the Classic Fairy Tale*. New York: Harcourt.

Blackaby, Susan. 2004. *The Emperor's New Clothes*. Mankato, MN: Picture Window Books.

Burton, Virginia Lee. 2004. *The Emperor's New Clothes*. New York: Sandpiper.

Davidson, Susanna, and Mike Gordon. 2005. *The Emperor's New Clothes*. Young Reading Gift Books. London: Usborne.

Demi. 2000. *The Emperor's New Clothes*. New York: McElderry Books.

Edgson, Alison. 2007. *Emperor's New Clothes*. Flip-Up Fairy Tales. Swindon, Wiltshire, UK: Child's Play.

John, Louise. 2011. *The Emperor's New Clothes*. Skylarks Series. Illustrated by Serena Curmi. London: Evans Brothers.

Lewis, Naomi, trans. 1999. *The Emperor's New Clothes*. Somerville, MA: Candlewick Press.

Rowitz, Mary. 1996. *The Emperor's New Clothes*. Lincolnwood, IL: Publications International.

Sedgwick, Marcus. 2004. *The Emperor's New Clothes*. Illustrated by Alison Jay. San Francisco: Chronicle Books.

Tharlet, Eve. 2000. *The Emperor's New Clothes*. New York: North-South Books.

Walz, Richard, and Rebecca Bondor. 1993. *The Emperor's New Clothes*. Little Golden Book. Racine, WI: Western Publishing.

The Emperor's New Clothes: I HAVE, WHO HAS Game

Directions: Cut all the cards apart. Each player gets one card. Begin with the question preceded by an asterisk (*). The student with the answer card responds.

I HAVE: A little child said the Emperor was wearing only his underwear. *WHO HAS: What did the Emperor value most?	I HAVE: The Emperor gave the weavers gold and provided them with weaving looms. WHO HAS: What did the Emperor tell his minister to do?
I HAVE: The Emperor valued his appearance more than anything else. WHO HAS: Why did the Emperor often walk in the streets of his kingdom?	I HAVE: The Emperor told the minister to go and see how the suit was coming along. WHO HAS: What did the minister see?
I HAVE: The Emperor wanted everyone to see his elegant attire. WHO HAS: When two impostors arrived at the palace, what did they claim to be?	I HAVE: The minister saw nothing but did not tell the Emperor. WHO HAS: What happened when the impostors brought the make-believe suit to the Emperor?
I HAVE: The impostors claimed to be weavers. WHO HAS: What did the impostors offer to make for the Emperor?	I HAVE: The Emperor pretended he could see the suit. WHO HAS: What did the Emperor proceed to do?
I HAVE: They offered to make a suit that could be seen only by those who were smart and good at their jobs. WHO HAS: What did the Emperor give the weavers?	I HAVE: The Emperor paraded before his people. WHO HAS: What did a little child say?

The Emperor's New Clothes: Library Treasure Hunt

Go to the children's nonfiction shelves. Look for each number on the spine of the books. What is each book about? That is the missing word. Write it on the line after the number. The player who finds all of the missing words first is the winner.

1. The Emperor's home was a 728.8. _____	2. The Emperor was very fond of 391. _____
3. The Emperor's shoes were made of the finest 675. _____	4. The Emperor gave the imposters a lot of 332.4. _____
5. The imposters pretended to be master 677. _____	6. There should be 328 against claiming to be what you are not. _____

Key: 1. castle; 2. clothing; 3. leather; 4. money; 5. weavers; 6. laws

The Emperor's New Clothes: Word Search

S	O	L	D	I	E	R	S	H	S
Y	E	N	O	M	S	E	O	H	O
P	L	S	A	P	E	M	I	O	O
M	O	T	S	O	H	P	S	S	N
M	I	N	I	S	T	E	R	R	M
L	A	S	M	T	O	R	E	R	D
S	L	O	A	E	L	O	V	H	O
S	O	S	M	R	C	R	A	E	O
L	R	I	T	S	I	I	E	P	M
E	D	A	R	A	P	M	W	N	P

Words to find:

Emperor   clothes   soldiers

imposters   money   looms

minister   weavers   parade

Little Match Girl

(The following can also be done orally, with the children raising their hands to respond.)

Find Someone Who!

Discover what your group has in common with the characters and places in *Little Match Girl*. Find a different name in the class or group for each item. The winner is the first to complete all eight items. The winner will then read each item and the person whose name is on each line will stand to verify that he or she can actually qualify for the item.

Find someone who . . .

1. Likes winter better than summer. _____

2. Has played outside on a cold day without a coat. _____

3. Visits his or her grandmother. _____

4. Knows what the word "poverty" means. _____

5. Can name a sad story. _____

6. Can name a story that has a castle. _____

7. Can say a word that rhymes with MATCH. _____

8. Lives or has lived in a big city. _____

Storyteller's Introduction to *Little Match Girl*

There are many film versions of *The Little Match Girl.* Some have other characters. Some have happy endings.

After reading the following and then watching the film, tell how the film is alike and different from the original Andersen tale told here in verse.

Holiday cheer
Christmas Eve
Ragged cloak
And torn sleeve
Child shivers
in the cold
selling matches
None sold.
Given orders
Must meet
Cruel father
Will beat
Heavy snow
Flakes fall
Finds nook
Stone wall.
Passers-by
Close eyes
And ignore
Child's cries.
Darkness falls
Comes night
Strikes match
For light
Sees vision
Flame released

Christmas tree
Sumptuous feast.
Sky glows
from afar
Shining bright
Falling star
Strikes match
And another
Sees smile
Dear Grandmother
Coming down
From skies
In arms
Child lies.
Morning comes
People look
See child
In the nook
Difficult
To reconcile
On face
Big smile
Murmured one
Man so wise
Child is now
In paradise.

Little Match Girl: The Films

Coronet, prod. 1978. *The Little Match Girl.* Puppet animated color film. 17 minutes. Ages 7–11. Follows the original story line closely. Distributed by Lucerne Media.

Hahn, Don, and Walt Disney Feature Animation, prods. 2006. *The Little Match Girl.* Short animated color film. Ages 7–10. Follows the original tale closely. Distributed by Buena Vista Home Entertainment.

NBC, prod. 1987. *The Little Match Girl.* Starring Maryedith Burrell, William Daniels, Haywood Dutton, Rue McClanahan. Live action color film. 60 minutes. Ages 8–adult. Varies considerably from the original tale with a modern setting and problems. Distributed by Good Times Home Video.

Sporn, Michael, prod. 2007. *Tales of Hans Christian Andersen: The Red Shoes/The Little Match Girl.* Voices of Diana Cherkas, Devon Collins, Ossie Davis, Edwun O'Neill. Animated color film. 60 minutes. Ages 7–12. Digresses from the original in both setting and ending. Distributed by Lucerrne Media. Available from Amazon.com and Barnes&Noble.com.

Free viewing on the Internet via YouTube: *Little Match Girl,* http://www.youtube.com/watch?v=jNxQcIZ6ji4, running time 10:25, ages 7–12; http://www.youtube.com/watch?v=yUSzQBaWq0Q, running time 6:41; and http://www.youtube.com/watch?v=NGKBUn7bMWw, running time 5:34.

Little Match Girl: The Books

Cloke, Rene, illus. 1983. *The Little Match Girl.* Sherwood Forest, UK: Award Publications.

Erickson, Jon, illus. 1989. *Little Match Girl.* New York: Gareth Stevens.

Gilmore, Stanley F., Jr. 2010. *The Little Match Girl.* Hamstead, MA: Old Line Publishing.

Hijikata, Shigemi, illus. 1967. *The Little Match Girl.* New York: Crown.

Isadora, Rachel. 2003. *The Little Match Girl.* New York: Scholastic.

Jose, Eduard. 1989. *Little Match Girl: A Classic Tale.* Illustrated by Francesc Rovira. North Mankato, MN: Child's World.

Kingsland, L. W. 1981. *Little Match Girl.* Los Angeles: K & W.

Pinkney, Jerry, illus. 2002. *The Little Match Girl.* New York: Phyllis Fogelman Books.

Robinson, Hilary. 2007. *The Little Match Girl.* Illustrated by S. McNicholas. London: Franklin Watts.

San Jose, Christine. 2002. *The Little Match Girl.* Honesdale, PA: Boyds Mill Press.

Little Match Girl: I HAVE, WHO HAS Game

Directions: Cut all the cards apart. Each player gets one card. Begin with the question preceded by an asterisk (*). The student with the answer card responds.

I HAVE: Passersby find the frozen child with a smile on her face. *WHO HAS: On what night of the year does the story take place?	I HAVE: The little girl lights matches to keep warm. WHO HAS: What does she see in the glow of the matches?
I HAVE: The story takes place on New Year's Eve. WHO HAS: Why is the little girl freezing on the streets?	I HAVE: She sees a Christmas tree and a table filled with food. WHO HAS: What is the meaning of the shooting star she sees?
I HAVE: She is freezing because she has been ordered to sell matches by her cruel father. WHO HAS: What will happen to her if she does not sell all the matches?	I HAVE: The shooting star means someone has died and gone to heaven. WHO HAS: What person does the little match girl see?
I HAVE: If she does not sell all the matches, she will be beaten by her father. WHO HAS: What does she do to escape the cold?	I HAVE: The little match girl sees her grandmother in a vision. WHO HAS: What does the grandmother do?
I HAVE: To escape the cold, she finds shelter by a wall. WHO HAS: What else does she do to keep warm?	I HAVE: The grandmother carries the child's soul to heaven. WHO HAS: What do passersby find the next morning?

Little Match Girl: Library Treasure Hunt

Go to the children's nonfiction shelves. Look for each number on the spine of the books. What is each book about? That is the missing word. Write it on the line after the number. The player who finds all of the missing words first is the winner.

1. Hans Christian Andersen is an author from 948.9. _____	2. In the glow of a match the little match girl saw a beautiful 582.16. _____
3. The table was piled with holiday 613.2. _____	4. The little match girl struck matches to keep warm from the 628.9. _____
5. Winter is one of the four 508.2. _____	6. The little match girl saw a shooting 523.8. _____

_____

Key: 1. Denmark; 2. tree; 3. food; 4. fire; 5. seasons; 6. star

Little Match Girl: Word Search

N	O	I	S	I	V	G
F	T	A	T	S	S	I
H	E	M	T	T	N	R
H	E	A	V	E	N	L
R	R	T	S	N	O	W
A	T	C	M	T	E	I
R	S	H	W	O	L	G

Words to find:

match	girl	snow
feast	star	heaven
vision	glow	street

The Little Mermaid

(The following can also be done orally, with the children raising their hands to respond.)

Find Someone Who!

Discover what your group has in common with the characters and places in *The Little Mermaid.* Find a different name in the class or group for each item. The winner is the first to complete all eight items. The winner will then read each item and the person whose name is on each line will stand to verify that he or she can actually qualify for the item.

Find someone who . . .

1. Can name a fairy tale with a witch.   _____

2. Has visited the ocean.   _____

3. Can name two ocean creatures.   _____

4. Can name another story with a prince.   _____

5. Has given up something to get something he or she really wanted.   _____

6. Knows what coral is.   _____

7. Can say a word that rhymes with SEA.   _____

8. Has a first name that begins with the letter A.   _____

Storyteller's Introduction to *The Little Mermaid*

Can be read as a poem or sung to "My Bonnie Lies Over the Ocean." Audience members add the missing words.

A mermaid looked over the ocean
To view all the world from above.
She saves a young prince from near-drowning
And with the prince she falls in _____. *(love)*

Chorus:
Lit-tle mer-maid
She goes to the Sea Witch, and there she begs
"If you'll help me
Then I'll trade my voice for two _____." *(legs)*

The Sea Witch sends her to the palace.
The mermaid has only one goal
That she and the prince will be married
Then she will have a human _____. *(soul)*

Chorus:
Lit-tle mer-maid
The king has decreed that the prince be _____. *(wed)*
Not you, mer-maid,
He'll marry a princess instead.

The mermaid is given a dagger
She's told how to use it and when.
The prince meets his death from the dagger
She'll be-come a mermaid again.

Chorus:
Lit-tle mer-maid
She picks up the knife and throws it away
Bro-ken hearted
The young prince will not die this _____. *(day)*

The mermaid returns to the ocean
Her body dissolves into foam
She now has turned into a spirit
And lives in a heavenly _____. *(home)*

The Little Mermaid: The Films

Allumination, prod. 2006. *The Little Mermaid.* Animated color film. 70 minutes. Ages 8–12. Follows the original Andersen story line. Distributed by UAV Corporation. Available from Amazon.com and Barnes&Noble.com.

Golden Films, prod. 1992. *The Little Mermaid.* Animated color film. 49 minutes. Ages 6–10. Nicely done film that follows the original story line. Distributed by Good Times Home Entertainment. Available from Amazon.com and Barnes&Noble.com.

Readers Digest with Potterton Productions, prods. 1974. *The Little Mermaid.* Narrated by Richard Chamberlain. Animated color film. 25 minutes. Ages 8–adult. Follows the story line of the original tale. Distributed by Pyramid Film and Video.

Walt Disney Studios, prod. 1989. *The Little Mermaid.* Voices of Buddy Hackett, Kenneth Mars, Pat Carroll. Animated musical color film. 82 minutes. Ages 4–12. Loosely follows the Andersen story line with many exceptions and a traditional Disney happy ending. Distributed by Buena Vista Home Video.

Free viewing on the Internet via YouTube: *The Little Mermaid: Ariel's Beginning,* http://www.youtube.com/watch?v=xhKESMmZJMs, running time 4:26, ages 5–10.

The Little Mermaid: The Books

Andersen, Hans Christian. 1981. *The Little Mermaid.* Illustrated by Michael Hague. New York: Henry Holt.

Andersen, Hans Christian. 1997. *The Little Mermaid.* New York: Hyperion.

Andersen, Hans Christian. 2003. *The Little Mermaid and Other Fairy Tales.* Evergreen Classics. Mineola, NY: Dover.

Andersen, Hans Christian. 2004. *The Little Mermaid.* Illustrated by Susan Blackaby. Mankato, MN: Picture Window Books.

Andersen, Hans Christian. 2005. *The Little Mermaid and Other Tales.* Book and Charm Series. New York: Harper Festival.

Andersen, Hans Christian. 2009. *The Little Mermaid.* New York: Pinnacle Books.

Edgar, Amy. 1999. *The Little Mermaid: A Read-Aloud Storybook.* White Plains, NY: Disney.

Hautzig, Deborah, and Darcy May. 1991. *The Little Mermaid.* New York: Random House.

Kahn, Sheryl. 1997. *Disney's the Little Mermaid.* N.p.: Mouse Works.

King, Enid C., and Brian Price Thomas. 1982. *The Little Mermaid.* New York: Penguin.

Santore, Charles. 1997. *The Little Mermaid.* New York: Random House.

Saunders, Katie, illus. 2006. *The Little Mermaid.* Berkhamsted, UK: Make Believe Ideas.

Stephen, Sarah Hines. 2002. *The Little Mermaid and Other Stories.* New York: Scholastic.

Zwerger, Lisbeth, illus. 2004. *The Little Mermaid.* New York: Penguin Young Readers Group.

The Little Mermaid: I HAVE, WHO HAS Game

Directions: Cut all the cards apart. Each player gets one card. Begin with the question preceded by an asterisk (*). The student with the answer card responds.

I HAVE: She finds freedom and a heavenly home. *WHO HAS: Where does the Little Mermaid live?	I HAVE: The Sea Witch gives the Little Mermaid legs in exchange for her voice. WHO HAS: What does the prince like most about the Little Mermaid?
I HAVE: She lives in the sea with her father the Sea King and her five sisters. WHO HAS: What does each sister get to do on her fifteenth birthday?	I HAVE: The prince likes to see her dance and to dance with her. WHO HAS: What does the prince's father order him to do?
I HAVE: On her fifteenth birthday each sister gets to swim to the surface and see the world. WHO HAS: What does the Little Mermaid see when it is her turn to go to the surface?	I HAVE: The prince's father orders him to marry a princess from another kingdom. WHO HAS: What do the Little Mermaid's sisters give her?
I HAVE: The Little Mermaid sees a ship and saves a prince from drowning. WHO HAS: What does the Little Mermaid wish for?	I HAVE: They give her a knife, and if she kills the prince, she will become a mermaid again. WHO HAS: What does the Little Mermaid do?
I HAVE: The Little Mermaid wishes to marry the prince and have a human soul. WHO HAS: Who makes it possible for the Little Mermaid to have legs?	I HAVE: She throws herself into the sea and is turned to foam. WHO HAS: What happens to the Little Mermaid?

The Little Mermaid: Library Treasure Hunt

Go to the children's nonfiction shelves. Look for each number on the spine of the books. What is each book about? That is the missing word. Write it on the line after the number. The player who finds all of the missing words first is the winner.

1. Hans Christian Andersen is an author from 948.9.	2. When the Little Mermaid first saw the prince, he was on a 387.2.
3. The ship was wrecked in a violent 551.55.	4. The prince liked to watch the Little Mermaid 792.8.
5. When the prince married, the Little Mermaid's 612.1 was broken.	6. The Sea Witch took the Little Mermaid's voice that sounded like 784.19.

Key: 1. Denmark; 2. ship; 3. storm; 4. dance; 5. heart; 6. music

The Little Mermaid: Word Search

S	P	I	C	S	P	D	P	R
P	S	R	E	T	S	I	S	M
I	H	D	I	R	C	A	P	D
D	P	M	R	N	N	M	I	A
E	S	R	P	O	C	R	H	T
H	C	T	I	W	A	E	S	A
H	S	T	O	N	A	M	S	N
O	O	R	W	R	C	R	M	S
P	R	W	T	D	M	E	S	P

Words to find:

mermaid	seawitch	sisters
ship	storm	prince
potion	princess	heart

The Nightingale

(The following can also be done orally, with the children raising their hands to respond.)

Find Someone Who!

Discover what your group has in common with the characters and places in *The Nightingale*. Find a different name in the class or group for each item. The winner is the first to complete all eight items. The winner will then read each item and the person whose name is on each line will stand to verify that he or she can actually qualify for the item.

Find someone who . . .

1. Can find China on a map.   _____

2. Can name two different birds.   _____

3. Has a mechanical toy that no longer works.   _____

4. Knows what the word "scoundrel" means.   _____

5. Has found a bird's nest.   _____

6. Knows what an emperor is.   _____

7. Can say a word that rhymes with SING.   _____

8. Has a pet bird.   _____

Storyteller's Introduction to *The Nightingale*

The audience responds at signals from the storyteller. A raised right hand signals the response, "That's good!" A raised left hand signals the response, "That's bad!"

Storyteller: The Emperor of China was walking in his garden when he heard the sound of a beautiful bird. The kitchen maid who was picking lettuce for the Emperor's dinner told him that the bird was a nightingale.

"Go and find the bird," the Emperor told the maid, "and tell it I shall welcome it as a guest at the royal palace."

Audience: That's good!

Storyteller: No, that was bad, for when the nightingale arrived at the palace it was caught and put into a golden cage and ordered to sing each day for the emperor.

Audience: That's bad!

Storyteller: Not really, for when a jeweled mechanical bird was given to the emperor he forgot all about the real nightingale and the kitchen maid let it escape back to the forest.

Audience: That's good!

Storyteller: It would have been good, except that the mechanical bird broke down and stopped singing and the emperor became very ill.

Audience: That's bad!

Storyteller: Only for a short time, for when the nightingale heard of the emperor's illness it flew to the palace and sang its sweetest songs.

Audience: That's good!

Storyteller: Yes, it was, for the emperor got well and the nightingale was free to fly throughout all of China and bring to the Emperor news of what she saw, which helped him to become a very wise ruler.

The Nightingale: The Films

Coronet, prod. 1984. *The Nightingale.* Color film animated with puppets. 16 minutes. Ages 5–10. Follows the traditional tale. Distributed by Coronet/MTI Film and Video.

Duvall, Shelley, prod. 1983. *The Nightingale.* Faerie Tale Theatre. Starring Mick Jagger, Bud Cort, Barbara Hershey. Live action color film. 54 minutes. Ages 8–adult. True to the traditional tale. Distributed by Fox Video.

Rabbit Ears Productions, prod. 1987. *The Emperor and the Nightingale.* Narrated by Glenn Close. Color film with limited animation. 40 minutes. Ages 6–12. Faithful to the original tale with musical background. Distributed by SVE/Triumph.

Winstar, prod. 1948. *The Emperor and the Nightingale.* Starring Boris Karloff, Jaromir Sobota, Helena Patockova. Live action film with puppet animation. 70 minutes. Ages 6–12. Follows the traditional tale, introduced by a young boy's dream. Distributed by Rembrandt Films.

Free audio stories available from Storynory (includes "The Nightingale"): http://storynory.com/.

The Nightingale: The Books

Andersen, Hans Christian. 1989. *The Nightingale.* South Norwalk, CT: Rabbit Ears.

Crook, Marie, and Angus McBride. 2000. *The Emperor and the Nightingale.* New York: Penguin.

Dalkey, Kara. 1991. *The Nightingale.* New York: Ace.

Dickins, Rosie, and Graham Philpot. 2007. *The Emperor and the Nightingale.* London: Usborne.

Gallaway, Morgana. 2009. *The Nightingale.* New York: Kensington Publishers.

Jose, Eduard. 1989. *The Emperor's Nightingale.* North Mankato, MN: Child's World.

Mitchell, Stephen. 2002. *The Nightingale.* Illustrated by Bagram Ibatoulline. Somerville, MA: Candlewick.

Oleynikov, Igor, illus. 2007. *The Nightingale.* Port Washington, NY: Purple Bear Books.

Pinkney, Jerry, illus. 2002. *The Nightingale.* New York: Dial.

Slater, Teddy. 1992. *The Emperor's Nightingale.* Disney Archives Series. White Plains, NY: Disney.

Waters, Fiona, and Paul Birkbeck. 1999. *The Emperor and the Nightingale.* New York: Bloomsbury Children's.

The Nightingale: I HAVE, WHO HAS Game

Directions: Cut all the cards apart. Each player gets one card. Begin with the question preceded by an asterisk (*). The student with the answer card responds.

I HAVE: The emperor gets well and asks the bird to travel the kingdom as his eyes and ears. *WHO HAS: What country does the Emperor rule?	I HAVE: A beautiful mechanical bird arrives as a gift to the emperor. WHO HAS: What happens to the nightingale when the mechanical bird replaces it?
I HAVE: The emperor rules China. WHO HAS: What beautiful sound does the emperor hear?	I HAVE: The nightingale is turned loose in the forest. WHO HAS: What happens to the mechanical bird?
I HAVE: The emperor hears the song of the nightingale. WHO HAS: What does the emperor order be done with the nightingale?	I HAVE: The mechanical bird malfunctions and stops singing. WHO HAS: What happens to the emperor?
I HAVE: The emperor orders the bird to be caught and brought to the palace. WHO HAS: What happens to the bird when it is caught and brought to the palace?	I HAVE: The emperor becomes seriously ill. WHO HAS: What is the nightingale asked to do?
I HAVE: The emperor puts the bird in a cage and orders it to sing every day. WHO HAS: What draws the emperor's attention away from the nightingale?	I HAVE: The nightingale is asked to come and sing for the emperor. WHO HAS: What happens when the nightingale comes to the palace and sings for the emperor?

The Nightingale: Library Treasure Hunt

Go to the children's nonfiction shelves. Look for each number on the spine of the books. What is each book about? That is the missing word. Write it on the line after the number. The player who finds all of the missing words first is the winner.

1. Hans Christian Andersen is an author from 948.9. _____	2. When the emperor first heard the nightingale, it was in the 577.3. _____
3. The emperor ruled the country of 951.05. _____	4. The mechanical bird was covered with 745.58. _____
5. The nightingale was a beautiful 598. _____	6. The nightingale made beautiful 784.19. _____

Key: 1. Denmark; 2. forest; 3. China; 4. jewels; 5. bird; 6. music

The Nightingale: Word Search

I	E	M	M	R	T	F	C	T
T	O	F	R	C	R	E	R	R
N	J	R	O	F	G	N	O	S
H	D	U	B	R	V	R	A	A
M	R	J	E	W	E	L	S	N
T	I	I	T	P	D	S	N	I
T	B	E	M	D	O	I	T	H
I	I	E	V	I	T	P	A	C
E	O	I	O	M	U	R	O	M

Words to find:

emperor	China	forest
bird	maid	song
jewels	court	captive

The Princess and the Pea

(The following can also be done orally, with the children raising their hands to respond.)

Find Someone Who!

Discover what your group has in common with the characters and places in *The Princess and the Pea*. Find a different name in the class or group for each item. The winner is the first to complete all eight items. The winner will then read each item and the person whose name is on each line will stand to verify that he or she can actually qualify for the item.

Find someone who . . .

1. Can name a fairy tale with a princess.   _____

2. Has gotten wet after being caught in
   the rain.   _____

3. Likes to play in the rain.   _____

4. Has planted peas in a garden.   _____

5. Has had trouble going to sleep.   _____

6. Can name a real queen.   _____

7. Can say three words that rhyme with PEA.   _____

8. Can name a word that means the same
   as the word "castle.   _____

Storyteller's Introduction to *The Princess and the Pea*

At a signal from the storyteller, the audience will repeat the last two lines of each verse.

Storyteller:
A young prince
searched
Far and wide
For a princess
To be his bride
Came home alone
Feeling sad
A real princess
Not to be had.

Audience:
A real princess
Not to be had.

Storyteller:
It rained one night
An awful storm
Those inside were
Safe from harm.
But underneath the
Thunder's roar
Came a knocking
At the door.

Audience:
Came a knocking
At the door.

Storyteller:
A real princess
Stood right there
Water streaming
From her hair.
Is she more real
Than the rest?
The Queen will put her
To the test.

Audience:
The Queen will put her
To the test.

Storyteller:
Queen laid upon
The bed a pea
Piled 20 mattresses
To see
If the pea
Could make a bump
If the girl
Could feel the lump.

Audience:
If the girl
Could feel the lump.

Storyteller:
The morning showed
A princess true
For the girl
Was black and blue.
The young prince
Searching far and wide
Had at last
Found his bride.

Audience:
Had at last
Found his bride.

The Princess and the Pea: The Films

Duvall, Shelley, prod. 1983. *The Princess and the Pea.* Faerie Tale Theatre. Starring Liza Minnelli, Tom Conti, Beatrice Straight. Live action color film. 60 minutes. Ages 6–12. Faithful to the original story with some additional characters. Distributed by Fox Video and Image Entertainment.

Swan Animation, prod. 1976. *The Princess and the Pea.* Animated color film. 89 minutes. Ages 6–12. Russian adaptation with English subtitles. Distributed by Visiplex Family Entertainment.

Free viewing on the Internet via YouTube: *The Princess and the Pea,* http://www.youtube.com/watch?v=mb_sG8qfv-I, running time 10:00.

The Princess and the Pea: The Books

Blackaby, Susan. 2004. *The Princess and the Pea.* Illustrated by Charlene DeLage. Mankato, MN: Picture Window Books.

Cech, John. 2007. *The Princess and the Pea.* Illustrated by Bernhard Oberdieck. New York: Sterling.

Child, Lauren, illus. 2006. *The Princess and the Pea.* New York: Hyperion.

Davidson, Susanna. 2007. *The Princess and the Pea.* Illustrated by Mike Gordon. London: Usborne.

Duntze, Dorothée, illus. 1985. *The Princess and the Pea.* New York: North-South Books.

Edwards, Pamela Duncan. 2010. *Princess Pigtoria and the Pea.* Illustrated by Henry Cole. London: Orchard Books.

Isadora, Rachel. 2007. *The Princess and the Pea.* New York: G. P. Putnam's Sons.

Lundell, Margo. 1994. *Princess and the Pea.* Little Golden Book. Racine, WI: Western Publishing.

Semelet, Camille, illus. 1999. *The Princess and the Pea.* New York: Abbeville.

Stockham, Jessica. 2010. *The Princess and the Pea.* Flip-Up Fairy Tales. North Mankato, MN: Child's Play.

Ziefert, Harriet. 1996. *The Princess and the Pea.* New York: Puffin Books.

The Princess and the Pea: I HAVE, WHO HAS Game

Directions: Cut all the cards apart. Each player gets one card. Begin with the question preceded by an asterisk (*). The student with the answer card responds.

I HAVE: The prince and princess were married and lived happily ever after. *WHO HAS: Why did a prince travel far and wide?	I HAVE: The girl claimed to be a real princess. WHO HAS: How did the queen put the girl to the test?
I HAVE: The prince was seeking a real princess to be his bride. WHO HAS: Why couldn't he find a real princess on his travels?	I HAVE: The queen piled 20 mattresses on top of a pea in the bed. WHO HAS: What else did the queen do?
I HAVE: There was something not quite right about each princess he met. WHO HAS: Who knocked at the castle door on a stormy night?	I HAVE: The queen piled twenty feather beds on top of the mattresses. WHO HAS: What happened the next morning?
I HAVE: A young girl knocked at the door on a stormy night. WHO HAS: What did the girl look like?	I HAVE: The girl was black and blue from lying on the hard pea. WHO HAS: How did this prove she was a real princess?
I HAVE: Water poured from her hair and her clothes. WHO HAS: What did the girl claim to be?	I HAVE: Only a real princess should have felt the pea. WHO HAS: What happened next?

The Princess and the Pea: Library Treasure Hunt

Go to the children's nonfiction shelves. Look for each number on the spine of the books. What is each book about? That is the missing word. Write it on the line after the number. The player who finds all of the missing words first is the winner.

1. Very dark 551.7 mean a storm is coming. _____	2. The real princess sought shelter from a 551.55. _____
3. The princess knocked on the 728.8 door. _____	4. The princess's 391 was all wet. _____
5. The princess had trouble getting to 612.8. _____	6. This story ended with a 392. _____

Key: 1. clouds; 2. storm; 3. castle; 4. clothing; 5. sleep; 6. wedding

The Princess and the Pea: Word Search

R	E	M	E	E	S	E	E
K	M	A	U	D	N	Q	C
I	S	T	O	R	M	U	N
N	U	T	O	U	A	B	I
G	E	R	S	N	U	E	R
S	S	E	C	N	I	R	P
S	U	S	U	B	E	D	T
M	E	S	R	Q	E	C	S

Words to find:

prince	princess	storm
king	mattress	queen
bed	museum	pea

The Snow Queen

(The following can also be done orally, with the children raising their hands to respond.)

Find Someone Who!

Discover what your group has in common with the characters and places in *The Snow Queen*. Find a different name in the class or group for each item. The winner is the first to complete all eight items. The winner will then read each item and the person whose name is on each line will stand to verify that he or she can actually qualify for the item.

Find someone who . . .

1. Knows what a troll is.   _____

2. Has grown flowers in a window box.   _____

3. Can sing a song about a flower.   _____

4. Likes winter better than summer.   _____

5. Has searched for something that has been
   lost.   _____

6. Has gone on a long journey.   _____

7. Has a first name that beings with either the
   letter G or the letter K.   _____

8. Had a friend who moved away.   _____

Storyteller's Introduction to *The Snow Queen*

Story Summary:

A splinter from an evil troll mirror gets in the boy Kay's eye and heart, making him evil and cruel. When winter comes, he attaches his sled to one driven by the evil Snow Queen. Her kiss makes him forget his friends and family. She takes Kay to her palace at the North Pole.

In the meantime, his friend Gerda goes to look for him. She crosses a magic river, meets a sorceress with a magic rose garden, and meets a crow who tells her of Kay's whereabouts. In her search she is helped by a prince and princess and captured by robbers but escapes and finally arrives at the Snow Queen's palace, which her prayers allow her to enter.

When Gerda finds Kay, her tears make the splinter in his eye and heart disappear and he becomes himself again. With the help of two women, they leave the land of the Snow Queen and return home to their grandmother.

Directions:

Distribute one story strip (see next page) to each of eight children. Challenge the group to line them up in an order they believe will tell the story. When they are done, each child reads his or her strip.

After hearing the story or seeing the film, ask the group to repeat the line-up activity. Is the second line-up the same as the first? Why or why not?

(1) A crow tells Gerda Kay's whereabouts.

(2) The next winter Kay goes with the cruel Snow Queen in her
    sled to her North Pole palace.

(3) Gerda is captured by robbers but then is freed and travels
    to the Snow Queen's palace.

(4) Kay becomes cruel when splinters from a troll mirror enter
    his heart and eye.

(5) They make their way home with the help of the reindeer,
    two women, and the robber girl.

(6) Kay and Gerda are friends who play together in a window
    box garden.

(7) Gerda searches for Kay and flees from the garden of a
    sorceress.

(8) Kay is saved from the Snow Queen by the power of Gerda's
    love.

Key: 6, 4, 2, 7, 1, 3, 8, 5

The Snow Queen: The Films

Duvall, Shelley, prod. 1984. *The Snow Queen*. Faerie Tale Theatre. Starring Lance Kerwin, Melissa Gilbert, Lee Remick. Live action color film. 60 minutes. Ages 6–12. Follows the plot but substitutes nonreligious words for a religious chant in the original tale. Distributed by Fox Video.

Ling, Chantal, Cherrylyn Brooks, David Mercer, Kathy Richardson, and Paul K. Joyce, prods. 2007. *The Snow Queen*. Voices of Pax Baldwin, Sydney White, Juliet Stevenson, Tiffany Knight, Colleen Williams. Animated color film. 56 minutes. Ages 8–14. Distributed by BBC Warner.

O'Connor, Matthew, Michael O'Connor, Robert Halmi Jr., and Robert Halmi Sr., prods. 2003. *The Snow Queen*. Starring Bridget Fonda, Jeremy Guilbaut, Chelsea Hobbs. Anamorphic, closed-captioned color film. 180 minutes. Ages 10–adult. Faithful to the original tale. Distributed by Lions Gate Media.

Free viewing on the Internet via YouTube: *The Snow Queen*, http://www.youtube.com/watch?v=X6hmAWzUs4g, running time 9:38.

The Snow Queen: The Books

Bell, Anthea, trans. 1985. *The Snow Queen*. Illustrated by Bernadette Watts. Saxonville, MA: Picture Book Studio.

Ehrlich, Amy. 2006. *The Snow Queen*. Illustrated by Susan Jeffers. New York: Dutton.

Engelbreit, Mary, illus. 1993. *The Snow Queen*. New York: Workman.

Kernaghan, Eileen. 2000. *The Snow Queen*. Saskatoon, SK, Canada: Thistledown Press.

Lewis, Naomi. 2007. *The Snow Queen*. Illustrated by Christian Birmingham. Somerville, MA: Candlewick.

Philip, Neil. 1989. *The Snow Queen: A Story in Seven Parts*. Illustrated by Sally Holmes. New York: Lothrop Lee and Shepard.

Ponsot, Marie, trans. 2001. *The Snow Queen and Other Tales*. New York: Golden Books.

Setterington, Ken. 2000. *Hans Christian Andersen's The Snow Queen: A Fairy Tale Told in Seven Stories*. Illustrated by Nelly Hofer and Ernst Hofer. Plattsburgh, NY: Tundra Books.

Sims, Lesley. 2005. *The Snow Queen*. Illustrated by Alan Marks. Tulsa, OK: EDC Publishing.

Tatarnikov, Pavel, illus. 2006. *The Snow Queen*. Port Washington, NY: Purple Bear Books.

Vinge, Joan D., illus. 2005. *The Snow Queen*. Rantoul, IL: SFBC Books.

The Snow Queen: I HAVE, WHO HAS Game

Directions: Cut all the cards apart. Each player gets one card. Begin with the question preceded by an asterisk (*). The student with the answer card responds.

I HAVE: The robber girl, two women, and the reindeer help the children to return home. *WHO HAS: Where do Gerda and Kay live and play?	I HAVE: Gerda learns that Kay has not drowned. WHO HAS: Why doesn't Gerda stay in the garden of eternal summer?
I HAVE: Gerda and Kay play in a window box garden in the city. WHO HAS: What happens to Kay?	I HAVE: A rosebush tells her that Kay is alive and a crow tells her he is in the Snow Queen's palace. WHO HAS: Who helps Gerda on her journey?
I HAVE: Troll mirror splinters get into Kay's heart and eyes. WHO HAS: How do the splinters affect Kay?	I HAVE: A prince and princess give Gerda warm clothes and a coach. WHO HAS: Who helps Gerda escape from the robbers?
I HAVE: Kay becomes cruel and sees those who love him as bad and ugly. WHO HAS: What happens to Kay when winter comes?	I HAVE: A robber girl frees Gerda, who goes to the Snow Queen's palace. WHO HAS: How does Gerda rescue Kay?
I HAVE: Kay is taken by the Snow Queen to her palace at the North Pole. WHO HAS: What does Gerda learn from the river?	I HAVE: The power of Gerda's love removes the splinters from Kay's eyes and heart. WHO HAS: Who helps the children to return home?

The Snow Queen: Library Treasure Hunt

Go to the children's nonfiction shelves. Look for each number on the spine of the books. What is each book about? That is the missing word. Write it on the line after the number. The player who finds all of the missing words first is the winner.

1. Gerda and Kay played in a window box 635. _____	2. The Snow Queen took Kay to her 728.8. _____
3. The Snow Queen lived at the 998. _____	4. Gerda searched for Kay all through the 508.2. _____
5. A splinter had given Kay a cruel 612.1. _____	6. The Snow Queen was really an evil 133.4. _____

Key: 1. garden; 2. castle; 3. North Pole; 4. seasons; 5. heart; 6. witch

The Snow Queen: Word Search

S	N	O	W	E	R	K	R
N	A	P	S	O	A	N	A
I	G	W	R	Y	T	E	A
R	I	I	A	D	R	E	G
Q	Q	N	E	G	O	U	A
O	R	T	T	A	L	Q	K
T	R	E	C	A	L	A	P
M	I	R	R	O	R	I	D

Words to find:

troll	mirror	Kay
Gerda	snow	queen
winter	palace	tears

Steadfast Tin Soldier

(The following can also be done orally, with the children raising their hands to respond.)

Find Someone Who!

Discover what your group has in common with the characters and places in *Steadfast Tin Soldier*. Find a different name in the class or group for each item. The winner is the first to complete all eight items. The winner will then read each item and the person whose name is on each line will stand to verify that he or she can actually qualify for the item.

Find someone who . . .

1. Has played with toy soldiers. _____

2. Has taken ballet lessons. _____

3. Has more than one doll. _____

4. Has lost a favorite toy. _____

5. Has gone swimming in the ocean. _____

6. Knows what a draught is. _____

7. Can say a word that rhymes with DANCE. _____

8. Can name four different toys. _____

Storyteller's Introduction to *Steadfast Tin Soldier*

At a signal from the storyteller, children repeat the lines in bold print.

Soldiers all
Twenty-five
Late at night
Come alive.
One tin soldier
Room surveyed
Saw below
A pretty maid.
Watching her
From above
Poor tin soldier
Fell in love.
For her heart
He could not beg
For he had
A missing leg.

Now dear children
Sad to tell
From a window
Soldier fell.
Found by boys
Made a boat
In went soldier
Off to float.
Paper boat
Danced up and down
Paper boat
Whirled 'round and 'round.

Filled with water
To the brink
Paper boat
Began to sink.
"Save me!" was
The soldier's wish
Swallowed by
A giant fish.
Fish was caught
On a hook

Purchased by
The family cook.
Fish cut open
Down the side
Found a soldier
Tucked inside.

Put the soldier
With the toys
Played with by
The girls and boys.
Imagine soldier's
Great surprise
When ballerina
Met his eyes.

Heart was filled
With greatest joy
Till picked up
By a boy.
Now he met
A fate most dire
Boy threw soldier
In the fire.
Gust of wind
Waiting there
Threw ballerina
In the air.
Into the fire
Not to part
The two became
A single heart.

Steadfast Tin Soldier: The Films

Disney, Roy E., and Donald W. Ernst, prods. 1999. *Fantasia 2000*. Animated full-color film. 75 minutes. Ages 6–adult. One portion of the film contains "The Steadfast Tin Soldier" with the ending changed to happy rather than sad. Distributed by Walt Disney Pictures.

Rabbit Ears Productions, prod. 1986. *The Steadfast Tin Soldier*. Narrated by Jeremy Irons. Iconographic color film. 30 minutes. Ages 6–12. Faithful to the original tale. Distributed by Random House Home Video.

Soderquist, Abe, prod. 1967. *The Staunch Tin Soldier*. Live action film with color animation. 27 minutes. Ages 4–8. Hans Christian Andersen tells the tale to children using objects from the story. Distributed by Britannica.

Free viewing on the Internet via YouTube: *The Steadfast Tin Soldier*, http://www.youtube.com/watch?v=VGwk0bb3qC8, running time 8:00.

Steadfast Tin Soldier: The Books

Archipova, Anastasiya. 1991. *The Steadfast Tin Soldier*. New York: Collins.

Blackaby, Susan. 2004. *The Steadfast Tin Soldier*. Illustrated by Charlene DeLage. Mankato, MN: Picture Window Books.

de Conno, Gianni, illus. 2006. *The Steadfast Tin Soldier*. Port Washington, NY: Purple Bear Books.

Delamare, David. 1999. *The Steadfast Tin Soldier*. New York: Barnes and Noble.

Digrazia, Thomas. 1981. *The Steadfast Tin Soldier*. Saddle River, NJ: Prentice Hall.

Jorgensen, David, illus. 2006. *The Steadfast Tin Soldier*. Madison, NC: Spotlight.

Jose, Eduard. 1989. *The Steadfast Tin Soldier: A Classic Tale*. North Mankato, MN: Child's World.

Lynch, P. J., illus. 2005. *The Steadfast Tin Soldier*. London: Andersen Press.

Mitchell, Adrian. 1996. *The Steadfast Tin Soldier*. New York: DK Publishing.

Riddell, Chris, illus. 1997. "The Steadfast Tin Soldier," in *The Swan's Stories*. Somerville, MA: Candlewick Press.

Seider, Tor. 1992. *The Steadfast Tin Soldier*. Illustrated by Fred Marcellino. New York: HarperCollins.

Steadfast Tin Soldier: I HAVE, WHO HAS Game

I HAVE: A gust of wind blew her into the fire beside the soldier, who melted in the shape of a heart. *WHO HAS: What was wrong with one tin soldier in a set of twenty-five?	I HAVE: Two boys put the soldier in a paper boat and sailed him down the gutter. WHO HAS: What happened when the boat sailed into the canal?
I HAVE: Even though he stood tall, one soldier in the set of twenty-five had only one leg. WHO HAS: What did the soldier see standing in a palace door?	I HAVE: The paper boat sank in the canal and the tin soldier was swallowed by a fish. WHO HAS: How was the tin soldier rescued from the belly of the fish?
I HAVE: He saw and fell in love with a beautiful ballerina. WHO HAS: What happened in the toy room late at night?	I HAVE: A cook cut open the belly when she prepared the fish for dinner. WHO HAS: What did the cook do when she found the tin soldier in the fish?
I HAVE: Late at night the toys came alive but the soldier did not speak to the ballerina. WHO HAS: What happened to the soldier the next morning?	I HAVE: The cook took the tin soldier to the toy room where he again saw the ballerina. WHO HAS: What did a child do with the tin soldier?
I HAVE: A puff of wind blew him out the window. WHO HAS: Who found the soldier and what did they do?	I HAVE: A child threw the soldier in the fire. WHO HAS: What happened to the ballerina?

Steadfast Tin Soldier: Library Treasure Hunt

Go to the children's nonfiction shelves. Look for each number on the spine of the books. What is each book about? That is the missing word. Write it on the line after the number. The player who finds all of the missing words first is the winner.

1. The soldier lived in a room full of 745.592. _____	2. The soldier was made of 546. _____
3. The ballerina loved to 792.8. _____	4. The soldier was swallowed by a 597. _____
5. A boy threw the soldier into a 628.9. _____	6. All that was left was the soldier's 612.1. _____

Key: 1. toys; 2. tin; 3. dance; 4. fish; 5. fire; 6. heart

Steadfast Tin Soldier: Word Search

D	C	H	A	A	E	E
A	A	L	E	T	M	A
N	S	N	Y	A	A	E
C	T	G	I	O	R	L
E	L	D	E	B	E	T
R	E	I	D	L	O	S
N	A	W	S	A	B	Y

Words to find:

soldier	legs	castle
swan	dancer	boy
boat	maiden	heart

Thumbelina

(The following can also be done orally, with the children raising their hands to respond.)

Find Someone Who!

Discover what your group has in common with the characters and places in *Thumbelina*. Find a different name in the class or group for each item. The winner is the first to complete all eight items. The winner will then read each item and the person whose name is on each line will stand to verify that he or she can actually qualify for the item.

Find someone who . . .

1. Can name three farm animals. _____

2. Has taken walnuts out of the shell. _____

3. Has a favorite flower. _____

4. Likes to catch fish. _____

5. Has played a trick on someone. _____

6. Has found a four leaf clover. _____

7. Can say a word that rhymes with TOAD. _____

8. Can tell where a mole lives. _____

Storyteller's Introduction to *Thumbelina*

Audience members practice the following refrain several times and repeat it at a signal from the storyteller. At the end, the audience repeats the final four lines.

Thumbelina   Where oh where
Sings a song.   Does she belong?

Storyteller:
A childless woman
Sad to tell
Begs a witch
To cast a spell.
The witch
Picks up
A kernel of corn
Says magic words
A child is born.

Audience:
Thumbelina
Sings a song.
Where oh where
Does she belong?

Storyteller:
Fair of face
Yet overall
The tiny child
Is one inch tall.
In a further
Episode
Captured by
An ugly toad
Thought the girl
Qualified
To become
The toad son's bride.
Fish set
Lily pad afloat
Sails down river
Like a boat.
Ugly cockroach
Can't decide

Should Thumbelina
Be his bride?

Audience:
Thumbelina
Sings a song.
Where oh where
Does she belong?

Storyteller:
Weather begins
Turning cold
Finds refuge in
A mouse household.
Mouse thinks the girl
Should be a bride
With blind mole
By her side.
Saved by swallow
Flies away
To a meadow.
Happy day!
Tiny people
Live in flowers
Sparkling rainbow
Summer showers.
Thumbelina
Fair of face
Has at last
Found her place.

Audience:
Thumbelina
Fair of face
Has at last
Found her place.

Thumbelina: The Films

Bluth, Don, prod. 2005. *Thumbelina*. Voices of Jodi Benson, Charo, Gary Imhoff. Animated full-color film. 86 minutes. Ages 4–10. Faithful to the original tale. Distributed by Fox Home Video.

Duvall, Shelley, prod. 1982. *Thumbelina*. Faerie Tale Theatre. Starring Carrie Fisher, William Katt, Burgess Meredith. Live action full-color film. 60 minutes. Ages 5–adult. Faithful to the original tale. Distributed by Fox Video.

Golden Films, prod. 1993. *Thumbelina*. Animated full-color film. 49 minutes. Ages 5–12. Considerable differences between this film and the original tale, with Thumbelina as a lighthouse keeper's daughter who sets off on a journey to seek help in repairing an aging dam. Distributed by Good Times Home Entertainment.

Hanna-Barbera and Hallmark, prods. 1990. *Thumbelina*. Narrated by Olivia Newton-John. Animated full-color film. 30 minutes. Ages 4–8. Faithful to the original tale, with some songs. Distributed by Hanna-Barbera Home Video.

Rabbit Ears Productions, prod. 1989. *Thumbelina*. Narrated by Kelly McGinnis. Full-color film with limited animation. 30 minutes. Ages 4–10. Faithful to the original tale. Distributed by SVS/Triumph.

Free viewing on the Internet via YouTube: *Thumbelina*, http://www.youtube.com/watch?v=FJ2Do2FPLsI, running time 7:13.

Thumbelina: The Books

Alderson, Brian. 2009. *Thumbelina*. Illustrated by Bagram Ibatoulline. Somerville, MA: Candlewick.

Blackaby, Susan. 2004. *Thumbelina*. Illustrated by Charlene DeLage. Mankato, MN: Picture Window Books.

Davidson, Susanna. 2009. *Thumbelina*. Illustrated by Petra Brown. London: Usborne.

Ehrlich, Amy. 2005. *Thumbelina*. Illustrated by Susan Jeffers. New York: Dutton Children's Books.

Falloon, Jane. 1997. *Thumbelina*. Illustrated by Emma Chichester Clark. New York: Margaret K. McElderry.

Graston, Arlene. 1997. *Thumbelina*. Illustrated by Erik Christian Haugaard. New York: Doubleday.

Greenway, Jennifer. 1992. *Thumbelina*. Illustrated by Robyn Officer. Kansas City, MO: Andrews McMeel.

Long, Sylvia. 2010. *Sylvia Long's Thumbelina*. San Francisco: Chronicle Books.

Mills, Lauren. 2005. *Thumbelina*. New York: Little, Brown and Company.

Palmer, Jan, illus. 1994. *Thumbelina*. New York: Golden Books/Western Publishing.

Pinkney, Brian. 2003. *Thumbelina*. New York: Greenwillow Books.

Sneed, Brad. 2004. *Thumbelina*. New York: Dial Books for Young Readers.

Thumbelina: I HAVE, WHO HAS Game

Directions: Cut all the cards apart. Each player gets one card. Begin with the question preceded by an asterisk (*). The student with the answer card responds.

I HAVE: The meadow is where her people live. *WHO HAS: What did the woman ask the witch to do?	I HAVE: The fish set the lily pad free. WHO HAS: What creature sees Thumbelina but decides not to marry her?
I HAVE: The woman asked the witch to give her a child. WHO HAS: From what did the witch create the child?	I HAVE: The cockroach decides not to marry Thumbelina. WHO HAS: Who gives Thumbelina shelter from the cold winter?
I HAVE: The witch created the child from a kernel of corn. WHO HAS: Who steals Thumbelina away?	I HAVE: A field mouse gives Thumbelina shelter from the cold winter. WHO HAS: Who does the field mouse want Thumbelina to marry?
I HAVE: An ugly toad steals Thumbelina as a bride for her son. WHO HAS: On what is Thumbelina held captive?	I HAVE: The field mouse want her to marry the blind mole. WHO HAS: How does Thumbelina arrive at the meadow of flowers?
I HAVE: Thumbelina is held captive on a lily pad. WHO HAS: Who sets the lily pad free to float down the river?	I HAVE: A swallow takes Thumbelina to the meadow. WHO HAS: What does Thumbelina find in the meadow?

Thumbelina: Library Treasure Hunt

Go to the children's nonfiction shelves. Look for each number on the spine of the books. What is each book about? That is the missing word. Write it on the line after the number. The player who finds all of the missing words first is the winner.

1. A 133.4 created Thumbelina from a kernel of corn. _____	2. The 597 cut the lily pad loose. _____
3. Thumbelina floated down the 577.6. _____	4. A mother 597.8 wanted Thumbelina to marry her son. _____
5. The meadow was full of 582.13. _____	6. This tale is a 398.2. _____

Key: 1. witch; 2. fish; 3. river; 4. toad; 5. wildflowers; 6. fairy tale

Thumbelina: Word Search

C	U	E	S	T	M	F	F	A	E
H	L	L	W	E	S	H	M	L	H
C	C	I	A	A	D	A	O	T	C
A	N	I	L	E	B	M	U	H	T
O	L	C	L	Y	M	O	S	H	I
R	H	O	O	O	P	I	E	O	W
K	I	M	W	U	F	A	L	I	R
C	H	A	A	O	B	L	D	E	A
O	R	O	H	W	O	T	O	S	N
C	U	O	E	A	I	S	Y	P	A

Words to find:

Thumbelina	witch	toad
lilypad	fish	cockroach
mouse	mole	swallow

The Ugly Duckling

(The following can also be done orally, with the children raising their hands to respond.)

Find Someone Who!

Discover what your group has in common with the characters and places in *The Ugly Duckling*. Find a different name in the class or group for each item. The winner is the first to complete all eight items. The winner will then read each item and the person whose name is on each line will stand to verify that he or she can actually qualify for the item.

Find someone who . . .

1. Has lived on a farm.   _____

2. Has given chicken feed to chickens.   _____

3. Has watched an egg hatch.   _____

4. Likes eggs for breakfast.   _____

5. Has moved to a new school.   _____

6. Knows what the word "despair" means.   _____

7. Can say a word that rhymes with FARM.   _____

8. Has seen someone plain become someone pretty.   _____

Storyteller's Introduction to *The Ugly Duckling*

Encourage children to predict the words in bold print.

One summer day
A mother duck
Heard her
Cracking eggs.
She stepped aside
And watched
As there emerged
Ten tiny **legs**.
All eggs but one
Had come apart
Five baby ducks
Stepped out.
And from that one
That giant egg
Emerged an
Ugly **lout**.
The ducks they bit
The hens they pecked
The ugly
Duckling's side.
And when a girl
Gave him a kick
He ran away
To **hide**.
All through the summer
All through fall
The duckling hid
From others.
He had no home
No place
No friends
No sisters and
No **brothers**.
The bitter cold
Of winter came
In ice he's
Frozen fast.
A farmer
Came along
And saw

The duckling
Breathe
His **last**.
He rescued him
And took him home
To his old
Greedy wife.
The duck awoke
And flew away
Fearful for
His **life**.
In spring he saw
The royal swans
Floating on
The lake.
He swam to them
And cried aloud
"My life is yours
to **take!**"
Just then below
The water's edge
He glimpsed
The unexpected.
For in the image
Mirrored there
He saw
A swan **reflected**.
And from the shore
He heard
The glowing
Praises
Of the crowd
And hid his head
For he
Had learned
A kind heart
Is not **proud**.

The Ugly Duckling: The Films

Starlight Video, prod. 2005. *The Ugly Duckling and Other Stories.* Animated full-color film. 78 minutes. Follows the original tale closely and includes other tales. Available from Amazon.com.

Timeless Tales, prod. 2005. *The Ugly Duckling.* Animated full-color film. 30 minutes. Ages 3–6. Follows the traditional tale's story line. Distributed by Turner Home Entertainment.

Free viewing on the Internet via YouTube: *Ugly Duckling*, http://www.youtube .com/watch?v=THmHFHBWQZc, running time 8:18.

The Ugly Duckling: The Books

Angaramo, Roberta, illus. 2006. *The Ugly Duckling.* Port Washington, NY: Purple Bear Books.

Braun, Sebastien. 2010. *The Ugly Duckling.* New York: Sterling.

Cauley, Lorinda Bryan. 1979. *The Ugly Duckling.* New York: Sandpiper.

Ingpen, Robert, illus. 2005. *The Ugly Duckling.* New York: Penguin.

Isadora, Rachel. 2009. *The Ugly Duckling.* New York: Putnam.

McCue, Lisa. 1989. *The Ugly Duckling.* Little Golden Book. New York: Golden Books/Western Publishing.

Mitchell, Stephen. 2008. *The Ugly Duckling.* Illustrated by Steve Johnson. Somerville, MA: Candlewick Press.

Packard, Mary. 1993. *The Ugly Duckling.* Timeless Tales from Hallmark. Kansas City, MO: Andrews and McMeel.

Pinkney, Jerry. 1999. *The Ugly Duckling.* New York: Morrow Junior Books.

Vainio, Pirkko. 2009. *The Ugly Duckling.* New York: North-South Books.

Watts, Bernadette. 2000. *The Ugly Duckling.* New York: North-South Books.

Ziefert, Harriet. 1997. *The Ugly Duckling.* Illustrated by Emily Bolam. New York: Puffin Books.

The Ugly Duckling: Let's Chant Activity for Younger Children

Put the writing pattern on chart paper and fill in the blank spaces with words from the children. If time permits share *Make Way for Ducklings* by Robert McCloskey.

Verse 1: Six words to describe ducks.

We like ducks!

_____ ducks
_____ ducks
_____ ducks
_____ ducks
_____ ducks
_____ ducks

These are just a few.

Verse 2: Six phrases to describe what they do.

Ducks that _____
Ducks that _____
Ducks that _____
Ducks that _____
Ducks that _____
Ducks that _____ too!

Shout aloud
See the crowd
We like ducks!

The Ugly Duckling: I HAVE, WHO HAS Game

Directions: Cut all the cards apart. Each player gets one card. Begin with the question preceded by an asterisk (*). The student with the answer card responds.

I HAVE: The duckling turned into a beautiful swan. *WHO HAS: How was one of Mother Duck's eggs different from the others?	I HAVE: Other creatures would have nothing to do with him. WHO HAS: What beautiful birds did the duckling see when fall came?
I HAVE: The egg was different because it took longer to open. WHO HAS: How was the duckling that hatched different from the others?	I HAVE: The duckling saw a flock of beautiful swans. WHO HAS: What happened to the duckling when winter came?
I HAVE: The duckling was bigger than the other ducks and was ugly. WHO HAS: What happened to the duckling in the barnyard?	I HAVE: The duckling became frozen in the ice. WHO HAS: Who rescued the duckling?
I HAVE: The other barnyard creatures attacked the duckling. WHO HAS: Why did the old woman ask the duckling to stay with her?	I HAVE: A peasant found the duckling and took it home. WHO HAS: What happened in the peasant's house?
I HAVE: The old woman thought the duckling might give her duck eggs. WHO HAS: What happened to the duckling when he left the woman's cottage?	I HAVE: The duckling upset the milk and butter tubs. WHO HAS: What happened to the duckling when spring came?

The Ugly Duckling: Library Treasure Hunt

Go to the children's nonfiction shelves. Look for each number on the spine of the books. What is each book about? That is the missing word. Write it on the line after the number. The player who finds all of the missing words first is the winner.

1. The ugly duckling began life on a 630.1. _____	2. Mother Duck took her new hatch-lings to the 363.6. _____
3. The hunting 636.7 chased the duckling. _____	4. The duckling thought he was a very ugly 598. _____
5. The duckling thought he might die of a broken 612.1. _____	6. Dark clouds in winter meant that 551.7 was coming. _____

Key: 1. farm; 2. water; 3. dog; 4. bird; 5. heart; 6. snow

The Ugly Duckling: Word Search

E	D	S	N	B	D	D	C
S	D	O	N	A	M	O	W
E	N	D	R	R	W	W	L
E	O	C	M	N	I	S	R
G	P	A	R	Y	N	M	B
D	G	D	R	A	T	N	W
P	O	E	A	R	E	H	G
C	H	I	L	D	R	E	N

Words to find:

barnyard	egg	geese
winter	dog	pond
woman	swan	children

PART III

FAIRY TALE BINGO

Fairy Tale Bingo Player Board

Directions: Each player must have a player board. The caller chooses one card from the Caller Cards (see next page) to read aloud. (Example: "Her foot size was exactly right.") The player makes a match by placing an X on the matching story square. The player who makes any six matches first is the winner.

1. CINDERELLA	2. BEAUTY AND BEAST	3. RAPUNZEL	4. THREE PIGS	5. HANSEL AND GRETEL
6. EMPEROR'S NEW CLOTHES	7. FROG PRINCE	8. JACK AND BEANSTALK	9. ELVES AND SHOEMAKER	10. ELEPHANT'S CHILD
11. PRINCESS AND PEA	12. RUMPEL-STILTSKIN	13. SNOW WHITE	14. SLEEPING BEAUTY	15. THREE BEARS
16. RED RIDING HOOD	17. PIED PIPER	18. LITTLE RED HEN	19. BREMEN TOWN MUSICIANS	20. GOLDEN GOOSE

Fairy Tale Bingo Caller Cards

Cut apart the cards, mix them up, and call them in any order. The player who makes six correct matches on his or her board is the winner.

1. Her foot size was exactly right.	**2.** Oh, dear Beast, don't die!	**3.** Her hair was like a long rope.	**4.** The brick house could not be blown down.	**5.** Look! A house made of candy!
6. His new clothes were beautiful and invisible.	**7.** A frog fetched her golden ball from a well.	**8.** Beans for our cow! Mother was angry.	**9.** Each night they did the cobbler's work.	**10.** Stop pulling my trunk!
11. I can feel the tiniest lump in my mattress.	**12.** I can spin straw into gold.	**13.** She had seven small friends.	**14.** A spinning wheel became a sleeping potion.	**15.** The strange cottage held a trio of surprises.
16. You don't look like my grandmother.	**17.** Rats, follow me!	**18.** Who will help me?	**19.** They made music to frighten robbers away.	**20.** Look! An egg of gold!

PART IV

PAPER BAG PUPPET PATTERNS

Paper Bag Puppets

Using the Puppets

Constructing and using paper bag puppets in acting out fairy tales can help children to:

- Gain skills in communication
- Develop oral facility
- Learn to concentrate on a task
- Focus their role-play activities
- Learn language skills through creative play
- Develop self-confidence
- Enjoy stories and literature (especially the reluctant readers)

The following puppet patterns can be used for more than one tale. For example, the mouse pattern is appropriate for use with both "The Lion and the Mouse" and "The Town Mouse and the Country Mouse"; the boy pattern can be used with many tales, such as "The Boy Who Cried Wolf," "The Golden Goose," "Hansel and Gretel," "Jack and the Beanstalk," and "Peter and the Wolf."

Making the Puppets

Materials needed:

- Small paper bag
- Scissors
- Glue
- Crayons, colored pencils, or markers

Steps to follow:

1. Color head with crayons, colored pencils, or markers and then cut out.
2. Cut out the lower part of the mouth.
3. Glue head to bottom of folded small paper lunch bag.
4. Line up corners of mouth, and glue under bottom edge of folded bag.

To operate the puppet, place your hand in the bag with your thumb aligned vertically against the side of your hand and move your fingers up and down in a good-bye motion.

Paper Bag Boy Puppet

Paper Bag Girl Puppet

Paper Bag Prince Puppet

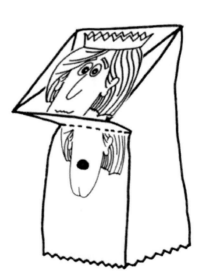

Paper Bag Princess Puppet

Paper Bag King Puppet

Paper Bag Queen Puppet

Paper Bag Giant Puppet

Paper Bag Witch Puppet

Paper Bag Bear Puppet

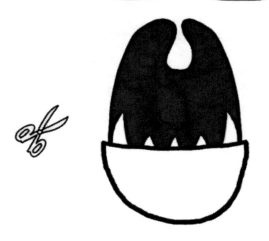

Paper Bag Frog Puppet

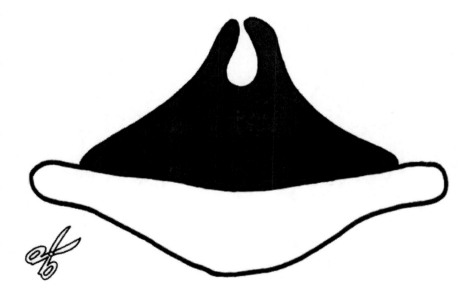

Paper Bag Lion Puppet

Paper Bag Mouse Puppet

Paper Bag Pig Puppet

Paper Bag Wolf Puppet

Author, Illustrator, and Title Index

About the Author and Illustrator

Nancy Polette is Professor of Education at Lindenwood University in St. Charles, Missouri. She is a former classroom teacher, Director of Library/Media Services and Gifted Programs in St. Louis County, and Director of the Lindenwood University Laboratory School. She is an in-demand conference speaker and the author of more than 100 professional books and ten children's books, including *Gifted or Goof-Off*, which won the Texas Legacy Award. *School Library Journal* describes Nancy as "an educator with imagination, creativity, and an appreciation for the intelligence of children."

Paul Dillon, a cartoonist/illustrator raised in Texas, received his degree in art from the University of Arkansas at Little Rock. He has been illustrating children's books and activity books for Nancy Polette since 1992. He lives in Maryland Heights, Missouri, with his wife, Carol.

2 1982 02809 8410

CPSIA information can be obtained at www.ICGtesting.com
Printed in the USA
LVOW030347170812

294716LV00002B/2/P

9 781555 707736